Bring in the
CLOWNS
a metaphor for ministry

Using the Spirit's creative gifts

Bring in the
CLOWNS

a metaphor for ministry

*To Elsie A—
+ Why Favorite Smile
Bud Frimoth*

Bud Frimoth

4/2/09

Pleasant Word
A Division of WINEPRESS PUBLISHING

Pleasant Word (a division of WinePress Publishing, PO Box 428, Enumclaw, WA 98022) functions only as book publisher. As such, the ultimate design, content, editorial accuracy, and views expressed or implied in this work are those of the author.

Unless otherwise noted, all Scriptures are taken from the Holy Bible, New International Version, Copyright © 1973, 1978, 1984 by the International Bible Society. Used by permission of Zondervan Publishing House. The "NIV" and "New International Version" trademarks are registered in the United States Patent and Trademark Office by International Bible Society.

Scripture references marked KJV are taken from the King James Version of the Bible.

Scripture references marked NASB are taken from the New American Standard Bible, © 1960, 1963, 1968, 1971, 1972, 1973, 1975, 1977 by The Lockman Foundation. Used by permission.

ISBN 1-4141-0772-2
Library of Congress Catalog Card Number: 2006928222

Dedication

Dedicated to
my loving companion of fifty-five years
Lenore—aka Wrinkles the Clown
and to our loving families who have put up
with the craziness that sometimes made
you wonder, "Am I related to them?"
To Margaret and Sharyn,
Chris, Barb, Aubrey, and Toby,
Todd, Brenda, Marshall, and Blake.

Deepest Appreciation
To Socataco the Clown - aka Floyd Shaffer
who first sent me on the clown road
and to Dennis Benson

who encouraged us to travel the different
roads of media and ministry.

Gratitude to a great seminary teacher
now beyond personal touch,
Dr. D. G. Stewart,
San Francisco Theological Seminary
San Anselmo, California

Table of Contents

Preface

What happens when there are two little girls, but only one pair of roller stakes?"

The answer was apparent when I caught the glimpse of the two laughing kids as they skated down the sidewalk. They had their arms around each other's shoulder as each wore one skate!

Creativity is the most basic, and most demanding of those who heed the call to respond to Christ. Yet, we often escape this beckoning of the Spirit by relegating creativity to a chosen few.

When we are called by the Spirit of God, we become a new creation in Christ. We are creative persons. Each of us is commanded to create the fresh and authentic forms of incarnation from what God has provided.

Bring in the Clowns—
A Metaphor for Ministry

Bud and Lenore Frimoth bear witness to this basic truth in this important and challenging book. Their gift to every Christian is the re-discovery of the power of transformation in our emerging future.

They have become vessels of ministry miracles by opening us to the power of God in the smallest, most basic, and most accessible moments of life.

This testimony is not really about the challenging incarnation of Christ in the art of clowning. Bud and Lenore are actually offering each and every person of faith a fresh mindset into what she or he can be and do as a Christian.

Bud and Lenore have been my spiritual kin during the past decades. We have stopped at moments along our journey of preaching and teaching along way. We have refreshed ourselves in the kinship of Christ.

The author beckons you to enter into a hopeful perspective of faithfulness. The stories of these pages will nurture and challenge you as you face the most exciting moment in the history of the faith now.

I invite you to join shoulders as we "skate" together into the emerging Kingdom of God with joy and expectation.

—Dennis C. Benson

Introduction

Over fifty years of ministry and eighty years of age and I'm still wondering what God wants from me. I think this is the story of many of us who have found our way into some forms of ministry, whether professionally or as laypersons. Do we have some guidelines we want to share?

My ministries continue in retirement. Dear friend Dennis Benson has laid upon me "to leave some crumbs behind so others will know the way." This book is an attempt to share both the extraordinary experiences I've been granted to explore, as well as the day-to-day wandering through life.

Nearly thirty years were in local church parishes. Overlapping some of that time I was privileged to spend time in a radio ministry with youth and young adults.

Bring in the Clowns—
A Metaphor for Ministry

That was over twenty-one years in radio. It led me into discovering the whole ministry of the caring and often-therapeutic clown as ministry.

Some basic ideas have hung out in reflection that I felt may be helpful to both lay and clergy. We're living in a different age from the one in which I began my ministries. Postmodern is the current favorite descriptive word.

Yet there are some principles of ministry, be they from the perspective of a clown ministry or lay parish worker, that give us encouragement and hope. We live in a stress-and-strife-activated world. What kinds of handles of caring can we as followers of the living Christ offer to that world?

Maybe you'll discover some of these anew as you skim through these pages. They are but a few from my shared ministry, and it would be my greatest desire that you discover more of your own. In the process, you may find that the clown metaphor speaks a new song in your heart. Perhaps it will even encourage you to risk taking steps in ministry that you never thought would be possible.

That is my prayer for each reader. Become what you are more fully as one of God's beloved children, even in adult bodies.

Chapter 1

Starting on the Floor— Discovering the Ordinariness of Ministry

What am I doing here, Floyd?"

"You're taking a little introduction to clowning."

"But I'm lying on the cold floor in a hotel room just trying to communicate with my body. All I feel is the hardness of the floor."

"It's where you're beginning to learn that clowning is more than just grease paint and a funny costume. Welcome."

That little encounter with Rev. Floyd Shaffer in 1976 during a media conference in Ft. Lauderdale, Florida, was the beginning of an odyssey of "always being the learner."

Here I was, a man with eight years of formal education beyond high school. It began with a Bachelors

Bring in the Clowns—
A Metaphor for Ministry

of Science in Education from Oregon State University, then four years at San Francisco Theological Seminary. There I received a Bachelor's of Divinity and a Masters in Christian Education.

Yet, I was on the hard floor, and Floyd was welcoming me to one of the most powerful experiences that ministry could offer. It became a pretty basic place to begin my further education in the journey of a million smiles.

"Clowning is a 'forever-becoming process,'" Floyd reminded me, and his words were ever so true. Nearly thirty years later, I'm still in that process. It sounds a lot like how I view the various parts of my ministries over the years as well. Clowning continues to be where I discover anew the wonders of God's creation. I have a new set of inner eyes to see where God intervenes. That intervention may be in others as well as inside of me.

It's strange how these little experiences provide "ahas" of wonder all the time. I really wasn't too sure how the church I was serving would receive such a thing as a clown service of worship, and then to also maintain a good theological view of the worship experience.

But I tested it out once I returned home to Portland, Oregon. Whenever I wanted to try some new creative experience in the church community, I would consult my wife Lenore.

"How would you think a clown service of worship would go over at Sunset Presbyterian Church?"

Starting on the Floor—Discovering the Ordinariness of Ministry

With a somewhat startled but knowing look she responded, "Tell me more."

"Well, there's a fellow in the Portland area who was trained by Floyd Shaffer. He said he would be willing to share a clown service of worship, but he'd need some help."

"And what is this help, may I ask?"

"He needs five people from the church to be clowns to help him. I've already have an OK from four of our youth but I need another one."

"Why not you?" she asked.

"I need to lead the rest of the service of worship. This will be the sermon for the day."

"Why are you looking at me?" Lenore questioned.

"I don't know where else to turn."

"Oh, all right. But after that Sunday we might as well start packing and look for another church to serve!" was her somewhat empathic response. Her naturally red hair almost emblazoned her words.

Thus the service of worship led by a clown happened.

We made many announcements of the service for about a month to prepare the congregation. Floyd had strongly urged us not to surprise a congregation. Let them have time to think and feel how they would respond.

Clowning is not something you pull as a surprise the first time it's offered. We've learned that lesson over and over again. When a congregation is not informed ahead of time, sometimes conflicts arise. We wanted to avoid that experience for the congregation.

By following Floyd's reasoned response, which was more of a "heart" than head trip, we prayed, made plans, and hoped for the best. Our Session had okayed the service. Then we offered members of the congregation an alternative to the clown service if this was a little too much for them to accept.

We took a chance. We told them it would be OK to attend worship at another congregation that Sunday. Now that took some real trust! The "floor" of our small congregation could have fallen if they all left us that Sunday.

To our surprise, on the Clown Sunday, it was one of the largest gatherings of the congregation and visitors we'd had. One of the elders even came wearing a shirt that had all kinds of circus animals on it. There were balloons and signs all over the sanctuary. The signs declared, "The Joy of the Lord is our Strength." People discovered that spirit as they entered the narthex as well.

We even gave people another option early in the service. If this was not what they were expecting in worship, there was a way out. During the first hymn they could slip out and no one would question their leaving. One man did just that, but we later learned he had a coughing problem. He managed to return before the clown segment occurred. To top it off, he was a visitor that Sunday morning!

Jerry, our clown friend, put the clown faces on all five participants before the service. They had gone through a quick practice with Jerry the night before. On Sunday morning he did what we call a "transformation" in front of the people. That is, he changed from Jerry into his clown. He put on makeup and changed his clothes. All the while, he used taped music to accompany his work.

At a given time, following his completed clown makeup, the other clowns hopped up from various hiding places in the sanctuary. They began tossing little Hershey chocolate kisses to the congregation.

Bring in the Clowns—
A Metaphor for Ministry

"That's when it really bit me," Lenore relates now. "I was taken by the possibility of clowning, whether it was in the church or somewhere else. I would never have expected it to affect a lot of what I also did later. However, our youngest teenage son, Todd, slid down in his pew when he saw his mother as a clown! Later, as an adult, he was responsible for providing us with a wide variety of clowning opportunities, including places outside the United States.

From the beginning, Floyd taught a special kind of clowning. He said that the other person was really the person on stage. We, as clowns, are the audience looking to respond to where they are. It is far more than an act.

Clowning showed me again how Jesus listened to others and then responded. Many of his stories must have been in response to questions from those around him. Take another look at the Beatitudes for instance. Someone must have asked, "What kind of life are you describing?" Jesus laid out those powerful descriptions of "Blessedness." That's another "floor" on which to grow a life of commitment to him.

Since that first clowning experience, I have found many areas where ministry can use the gifts of listening with the "ears of the heart" that clowns helped me discover. Ministry became even more a listening rather than a telling experience.

Starting on the Floor—Discovering the Ordinariness of Ministry

Essentially, that's how our journey of mirroring the clown began and continues. But we always need to be responsive to the incredible resourcefulness of our Creator.

In the first chapter of Genesis, it speaks of earth as being without form, and darkness was all around. Then the Spirit came and breathed upon that darkness and brought forth light. One can almost imagine that happening. Remember starting a campfire with one tiny match? Then you saw flame rise with color and warmth to embrace everyone around it, revealing a kind of Genesis experience.

Creation is still going on. One of the hardest lessons we all come to learn is that opportunities for serendipities occur in the oddest and some of the most familiar places. That breath (Hebrew *ruach* and Greek *pneuma*) was blowing on a tiny spark. Mine started on the cold motel floor.

This caused me to remember my first taste of the circus. It happened in junior high school. (That's what we called it when I was a youngster.) I was part of a play that included the circus. All I can remember is that my part was to be one of the boys trying to sneak into the circus tent. But being rather broad beamed, I got stuck trying to get in free.

All of me that was left showing on the stage was the large "back of my lap" under the curtain. No prat-fall...

just the "prat." Again on the floor! Little did I know that being a clown was in my genes someplace!

Maybe it was because one of the greatest clowns of the circus, Felix Adler, was from my hometown of Clinton, Iowa. Maybe some osmosis from him somehow slipped into my genes.

Maybe it came from my father who had been an aviator in WWI. On the back of his discharge papers were several telling statements.

"Flying hours solo - 743; Accidents: One; Forced landings: 13; Grounded by orders: 17 times. Reasons: Bad judgment, careless landings, reckless, too prone to take chances. Courage under stress: Excellent; Fellowship: Excellent. We grade this man and recommend him to Commission as 2nd Lt. in the United States Air Force."

However, he never continued his flying nor took me airborne in a plane. Maybe it was just as well for both of us. But the genes of being open to new "floors" certainly came from him. After all, he had immigrated to the United States as a young adult in 1913, then volunteered for the military service as well. Dad was "flying" for his dream of a new life in the U.S.A.

How clowning has affected
our married life

Lenore and I have been married more than fifty-four years. Half of them have been spent doing clowning

Starting on the Floor—Discovering the Ordinariness of Ministry

Bring in the Clowns—
A Metaphor for Ministry

as a supplemental ministry of mirth and wholeness. The encounters we've had revealed another avenue of ministry. As good friend and sister clown, Mary Ann Harty, put it, "Mirroring what another is feeling—that is the mark of the clown." That's also what ministry is about as well.

One of the advantages of being older is that you may be able to see things from a different perspective. But along with perspective you might also relate to the comment: "I'm over the hill, but I don't ever remember getting to the top." Who knows when you've reached the pinnacle of ministry or what new skills you might learn?

Why is it that we in ministry so easily lose our ability to be open to serendipities? It's like stopping to watch a butterfly dance from flower to flower, a simple reminder of momentary beauty and a life of looking for what is beautiful. Certainly the butterfly saw all the flowers and the colors that attracted her. She knew where to find the nectar she wanted.

Clowning has taught us to look for the nectar, God's delightful opportunities to lift the life of another or be lifted by that life. Some serendipities are remembered years after they happened.

When I was an eighteen-year-old soldier in WWII, on my first night of combat I was put on guard duty. All around us heavy fighting had been going on and our

Starting on the Floor—Discovering the Ordinariness of Ministry

artillery unit was positioned on several hillsides. German troops and tanks were not far away.

As I stood guard, I was hoping against hope I wouldn't have to be challenged by someone coming out of the dark, especially if he were unable to repeat the password for the night. Yet even during that night, I also noted the clear sky above. The radiant stars gave a surreal touch to the scene.

It also was then that I decided upon the name of my first son. I wasn't married or even had a serious girl friend. I was thinking pretty adult thoughts for a fuzz-bearded teenage soldier. That first son's name would be Christen. It was the combination of two grandfathers' first names: Christian and Chresten. Only years later did I discover that my Danish great-grandfather's name was Christen as well. Twelve years later, that son was born—on the Fourth of July!

On that frigid February night on a hillside in Germany, a serendipity occurred and I didn't know it. Sometimes that's how ministry occurs. We often miss early evidences of the work of the Holy Spirit because we don't acknowledge what we've been given.

Later in the war, I was more deeply involved in combat. There I discovered the taste and the smells of awesome destruction. Not just of buildings, but of lives. I felt like a number of former servicemen who later said of their experience, "There's got to be a better way."

Bring in the Clowns—
A Metaphor for Ministry

It was out of that experience of the awfulness of war that I ultimately moved my way into a helping profession. First was to be a high school teacher, and later I decided for the pastoral ministry in the Presbyterian Church in the United States. The Holy Spirit continued to work deep within my soul and energized my spirit to move on.

We Presbyterians are given to many words, and rightly so. It's part of our heritage from the days of the Reformation. The two great Johns in our tradition, Calvin and Knox, laid out thoughtful and erudite interpretations of the meaning and ministry of Christians. We need that construct for guidance, along with the Scriptures.

But there's another dimension we often skip—discovering the ordinariness of life. Like the flittering butterfly or a gorgeous sunset to which we may slip a glance. But we fail to absorb their message of hope and assurance that God still thinks we're worth saving. Every birth of a child is God's reminder that the Lord hasn't given up on the human race.

There are times when we need to get down on the floor and realize the sound foundations we have. It's a basic look at Scriptures from ground level up. We often do that when we are in a church camp. We spend time exploring the world around us. Somehow, as we "mature," we forget to get down on our knees and explore the world that lies beneath our feet.

Starting on the Floor—Discovering the Ordinariness of Ministry

I remember a day camp training session. It was held in the early days of the Presbyterian Ghost Ranch retreat center in New Mexico. We were among the first to use the facilities. A group of about twenty-five of us from all over the United States arrived to share in the training.

One of the wonder-filled teachers was noted camp leader, Maurice "T" Bone. There were many down-on-our-knees experiences we were asked to accomplish. One was to take a one square foot of ground and explore it. "T-Bone" asked us to list what we discovered.

We must have been quite a sight, hunched over on our knees, pulling out magnifying glasses, then scraping away little clumps of weeds. But we did discover all kinds of tiny bits of life and wonder. All on the "floor" we called the earth.

Another leader asked us to look all around us, especially at colorful New Mexico soils. She had us go out with little plastic pill bottles. We carefully placed in layered samples of the different colored strata of soil we discovered. I still have one of them on a file cabinet. It was basic, down-to-earth awareness. How much more earthy can one be?

What both of these leaders taught us was another way to stop and smell the roses. It was to be observant and take the time to let yourself be. That's right, just "be." On the ground floor you can begin to educate yourself to the wonders that surround you each day. God is constantly, literally throwing gifts at our feet. They become reminders of discovering grace in the ordinariness of life around us.

It is then that we begin to learn how to do something with what we have observed. "Being" then becomes the prelude to doing. To "be" is to have the floor in place from which to move. From there, the Spirit of caring leads us.

GRACE NOTES FROM OUR DAUGHTER'S WORK

Following college, our daughter Margaret was doing counseling with girls and women. They are women who had been abused—sexually, verbally, mentally, and physically. Some single and group counseling sessions were appropriate. Headway was made in helping those abused to move on with their lives. But she felt there needed to be something more. Something that would affirm each person that she was lovable and accepted beyond what had happened to her.

Beginning where they were, she brought together a group of women. They were sensitive to the needs of young abused girls. Some of the women had been abused during their lives so they could readily relate to the girls. But they had moved on in their healing. Thus new forms of good memories could begin so that the girls could continue to move on with their lives.

Out of many discussions, a plan was formulated. A camp for these girls—a "safe" camp, a place where they could allow themselves to be open would be an

Starting on the Floor—Discovering the Ordinariness of Ministry

opportunity to not feel the need to constantly protect themselves from harm, real or imagined. Thus a special camp was born. An acronym that voiced what the camp would be was born. VOCA—Victory Over Child Abuse.

VOCA camp started because the weekly girls group Margaret was working with had a concern. They were the state of Oregon Sexual Abuse group of girls. They asked if there was something more.

"Once a week is great," one said, "but about the time I'm ready to talk, it's time to go!"

Their sessions each week were an hour and a half.

From that "floor" experience, i.e. the very ground where these girls lived, came the basic plan and philosophy for the VOCA camp.

"We believe," Margaret indicates, "that healing is possible and survivors of abuse know what they need to heal. That's the ground floor experience. We intentionally create safety. Often, it is the child who also teaches an adult 'buddy,' and the teaching is welcomed. This allows the intuitive to flow. We seek to empower the children, and this is often done through their 'safe' buddy. The so-called powerless child becomes the provider of intuitive power to the adult buddy."

VOCA camp became a three-to-four-day camp experience. Specially trained adult "buddies" would be with each individual child during the period of the camp. They ate together, slept in the same cabin, went fishing, swimming, and did crafts together.

Bring in the Clowns—
A Metaphor for Ministry

Food was available twenty-four hours a day, things like fruit, cereal, yogurt, and hot chocolate. Abused children are often refused this in their homes as part of their "punishment." At VOCA camp the buddy and the child could go to the cookhouse anytime day or night.

At the same time, a special cabin was designated as a "safe" cabin. It was where anyone at the camp, counselor as well as camper, could go if she needed more time with another person.

For many of the girls, VOCA camp was one of the first experiences they had ever had where they could "let loose" and be the persons who was often locked up inside themselves. A reminder of what Margaret had said about VOCA camp being an "intentionally created safe" place.

At the first camp, during a time for crafts, one of the children drew a marvelous picture. It was of a beautiful rainbow, a large tree, flowers, and a brightly beaming sun. She titled the drawing, The Sunshine Starts Here. She had found safe acceptance of her as a person. That title has become the motto and logo for the camp since 1988.

VOCA found its floor in the lives of the young girls. It now has expanded to have another three-day camp for abused boys. The buddies for all of the camps go through a thorough screening. That's so that no predators find their way into the leadership. The extensive training—up to forty hours—is required for the buddies.

Starting on the Floor—Discovering the Ordinariness of Ministry

All of them are volunteers from their community in the Astoria, Oregon area.

Community leaders, businesses, churches, and social groups in the area have helped to make this special camp a reality over the years. Like most programs of this sort, there is a constant struggle to find adequate funding for current programs that now go beyond the camp itself. Campers have other opportunities during the year for activities. Local social agencies are also involved in supporting this community effort.

This all began with some abused children with an idea, a dream, but also with adults having the courage to put legs, arms, brains, and work into making it become a reality. They built on the floor they discovered. It all began in the ordinariness of life, even if it had been a disorderly experience of those abused.

By listening to those on the "floor," the abused children, the organizing group of adults were able to build an ongoing experience of healing. The survivors knew what they needed for healing.

Some of the first campers are now old enough to be among the new buddies, bringing full circle to the basic idea of being a person worthy of living. That's pretty basic. One might even call it the floor on which one can build a realizable life. Some girls have graduated into helping professions.

Not only is the camp continuing, but has expanded to a mentoring project as well. The Mentor Project is a year-round program that provides one-to-one support like that experienced in the camp. The organization that directs both VOCA camp and the Mentor Project is appropriately called The Healing Circle.

My first experience as a clown was hardly what I had expected. My body lying on the hard, cold motel room floor where the only way to move was up. Margaret made that same move from her "floor."

A COUPLE OF SCRIPTURAL CONSIDERATIONS

Check Jesus' healing of the man at the sheep gate in Jerusalem (John 5:1-18). The unnamed man had been there thirty-eight years seeking healing. Jesus saw that the man's illness was more than physical, so simply asked him, "Do you want to be healed?"

The man quibbled a little about no one getting him in the pool of water called Bethsaida when it was stirred up. Someone always beat him into the water. But Jesus saw through his excuse. Thirty-eight years was a long time to wait for a cure if it was really there. So he challenged the man to get up and take his mat with him.

The difficulty was in getting the man to see where his "floor" of illness lay. Jesus cut through the man's sickness. He gave him a reason to get up off the floor, mat and all. The man knew where healing came from—not just from Jesus, but from identifying his own need to get well.

Starting on the Floor—Discovering the Ordinariness of Ministry

Jesus ran into trouble, because the healing occurred on the Sabbath. The religious folk of his day had their own "floor," and it wasn't the same as that on which Jesus stood. It was the challenge of faith over laws. Jesus chose to go with faith, and the man was able to rise.

In Matthew 20:29-34, Jesus was leaving Jericho and two blind men called out to him for healing. Everyone around them told them to "shut up!" But Jesus asked what they wanted from him. "Lord, let our eyes be opened." And they were. Jesus created his own safe space.

No pretenses on either Jesus' or the men's parts. Jesus didn't ask of them any theologically couched questions about salvation. He started where they were and brought them sight. What happened? With new eyes they also "followed him." Jesus discovered their "floor," and then the two men took the opportunity to get off that ground and literally move on.

Check your experiences: Where did you begin your search for identity as a person? What kind of "floor" did you live upon? Where in the ordinariness of your own experiences did you have that "aha" sensation? Or like many of us, did you just slough it off at first? What kept pestering you to reconsider the direction of your life? After all, ministry always starts on the floor of life. Call it the earth, or as Dr. Paul Tillich taught us, "the ground of our being." I'm only now beginning to realize how important that ground has been for me. A powerful seed

was planted in it, and the growth came by the nurturing
Spirit. Lenore has hers:

> My wife is a bit crazy.
> She looks out on our yard
> And sees yellow lights—
> They're "calling" her to action.
> Those "grandchildren's flowers"
> She seeks to find
> Are simply the dandelion weeds.
> She knows she cannot get them all,
> But persistence and determination
> Allows her activity
> On this "ground" of her being...
> Watch out little weeds...she's coming!
> She wants a clean base
> For her lawn.

Rediscovering your floor is the basic first step. Consider these ideas for reflection before moving on:

1. When were you first aware that there was more
    to your life than just earning a living? Or are you
    still at that place?
2. Can you remember incidents of encouragement
    that touched you deep inside, even though you
    weren't aware of where they came from?
3. What were some of the first nudges of the Holy
    Spirit that gave you a sense that you were being

"called" to a different vocation? How did you feel about that experience, and what did you do with it?

4. Who were some of the first persons who influenced you to consider any form of ministry? (That includes those beyond being a pastor. It may mean teaching, dentistry, social workers, doctors, nurses, or any of the helping professions.)

5. Remember, Jesus was born in a stable, most likely with animals being present. It was a basic place from which his parents had to later move. What part did his family's low social standings play in his ministry? How do you think that "floor" affected how he reached out to others?

Raise up your internal antennas of the spirit. Think of the persons whom God has been using to encourage you to become the person you were meant to become. Have you ever taken the opportunity to write a note of appreciation for their encouragement? Now would be a good time!

We'll look at what is built on that "experiential" floor in the next chapter.

Chapter 2

Flawed Faces— Discovering Your Kind of Ministry

One of the first experiences you have with clowning is to determine what kind of clown face you will have. This usually determines what kind of clown persona you'll take on. If you look in a book that features faces of clowns, you will soon discover there are as many types of clowns as there are faces. But that shouldn't deter you.

Generally speaking, there are three basic types. White-faced, Auguste, and Character, which would include Emmett Kelly's famous "Willie the Tramp" clown. There are as many variations as faces in all three of these. Sport and school-team mascots are usually a different genre.

Each of these basic clown types has a reflection of personality. The white-faced clown is thought to be a happy kind of clown. This is the joyous, happy-go-lucky childlike clown.

For Lenore, this fit her personality, and she has continued to grow into it over the years. She has a knack for being playful and relates well with children of all ages and sizes. Add to this her clown name: "Wrinkles." Some of her female friends who were also in the late forties questioned her choice. But Lenore said, "When I turned fifty, I decided to become a clown."

The only difficulty with that statement was that she was only forty-nine at the time. But she loved the wrinkles that had come to her face. They represented years of child bearing and rearing. Crows feet at her eyes reflect years of smiles her family has brought her. However, when she sees advertisements in the newspapers about "getting rid of wrinkles," she puts on a little pout!

An Auguste clown is the outlandish clown. Everything is exaggerated. Often the face is elongated by a special wig with lots of hair and possibly a tiny hat on top. The face has large markings over the eyes, and the mouth is made larger than real life. This kind of clown could stumble over a shadow on the ground, but always gets up. He or she carries on in spite of everything.

Character clowns come in all kinds and shapes. When we first started clowning in the late 1970s, the Tramp clown was basically the only one in this category.

This is a sad-faced clown with blackened beard, white around the mouth and eyes, as well as rosy cheeks.

Flawed Faces—Discovering Your Kind of Ministry

This was to give the impression that he or she might have been really down on their luck. Sometime a red sponge nose is added. The clothing is tacky and often ripped with patches. You can feel absolute disgust for this

Bring in the Clowns—
A Metaphor for Ministry

low-life person, or possibly deep sympathy. However, that's the character that struck me the most at first.

I chose a strange name for my clown—"Doolotz," pronounced like "do lots." The basic idea came from the New Testament Greek word "doulos" which means servant. The servant role is not slavery, but one chosen to be available for others. Doolotz has done that for me for many years.

Flawed Faces—Discovering Your Kind of Ministry

However, I also have a second clown that was developed nearly ten years ago. Usually, you have just one type of clown and work to develop its character. But this one came out of a difficult experience in my life.

In 1995 I was doing my morning exercises in our basement when I experienced pain running down my left arm to a degree I'd never had before. I came upstairs and crawled into my favorite lounge chair. I told Lenore that I was sicker than I'd ever been. She called 911. A little later I had one of those very expensive "taxi" rides in the back of an ambulance.

Bypass heart surgery was needed to remedy my condition. During my hospital time a dear clown friend came to visit me. Albert Alter arrived on the cardiac floor carrying balloons. They were allowed in the hospital at that time because awareness of the latex allergies was not a concern.

Albert carried those partially-deflated balloons down the hallway, and I could hear laughter following him. When he arrived in my room, he offered his wonderful gift. It was more than the balloons. That gift was himself.

As I was recovering from surgery, I told Lenore, "We've got to go back to the hospital as clowns." The staff at Providence Portland Hospital and the cardiac ward had been very gracious and caring. I wanted to repay them. Becoming a caring clown was one way.

Bring in the Clowns—
A Metaphor for Ministry

Lenore's eyes rolled and she took a deep breath. Her head shook from side to side. But she knew that this plodding Dane would want to carry on. I had learned that laughter, smiles, and simple humor brought healing, even if it was only for a limited time.

Consequently, I decided that a Tramp clown would not be appropriate. There's enough sadness and concerns in the hospital. Patients don't need to have more of that thrust upon them. As a result I developed "Zyppurr" the clown. Zyppurr is pronounced "zipper." That's what we heart patients call the scar down the middle of our chests from surgery.

Zyppurr is a mix of white face and Auguste. The most outlandish part of Zyppurr's costume is a wonderful Dutch Boy yellow wig. Lenore made a costume that used material with lots of little hearts on them. I was ready to go back to the hospital. How it has gone will be described later.

What I have learned is that my flawed and wounded cardiovascular system could still function. I could carry on. Lenore has been through sessions with two types of cancer, so we knew our bodies can continue to work.

In determining what kind of clown you want to become, you have to look seriously and humorously at your face. Many of us men are a bit self-conscious about doing that. We'll do our shaving, combing of our hair, and other head treatments. Occasionally, when we think no one is looking, we might do serious and humorous poses for our own delight!

Flawed Faces—Discovering
Your Kind of Ministry

One of the first things we notice is that no face is perfect. There are flaws of all kinds that you may have forgotten. Symbolically, our face is a reminder that we are all imperfect—and that is OK.

The first time I put on my clown face was in that Florida hotel. Man-o-man it was ugly. Like many who put on grease paint the first time, you want to experiment. I had made a partially white face. Then to be clever, I added what turned out to be a horrible blue mouth spread beyond my lower lip. I didn't want to be a black-bearded clown, so I became a blue beard. When we teach clowning classes, I show my picture of this to students. It is helpful once they have "tried on their new faces." Flawed faces can change.

For thirty years the face of Doolotz is still not exactly the same each time. It's close, but some parts of my face have changed. This happens especially as we age. My wrinkles become very apparent when I do Zyppurr the white-faced clown. A family member of a hospital patient recognized the problem. He said to Zyppurr, "You're too old to be clowning!"

A little later, the same man saw us in action in his family member's hospital room. He apologized and said he didn't know what kind of clowning we did. That happened several years ago, but Wrinkles and I have continued.

Although we have many similarities with circus clowns, we have specific differences. We are part of what

Bring in the Clowns—
A Metaphor for Ministry

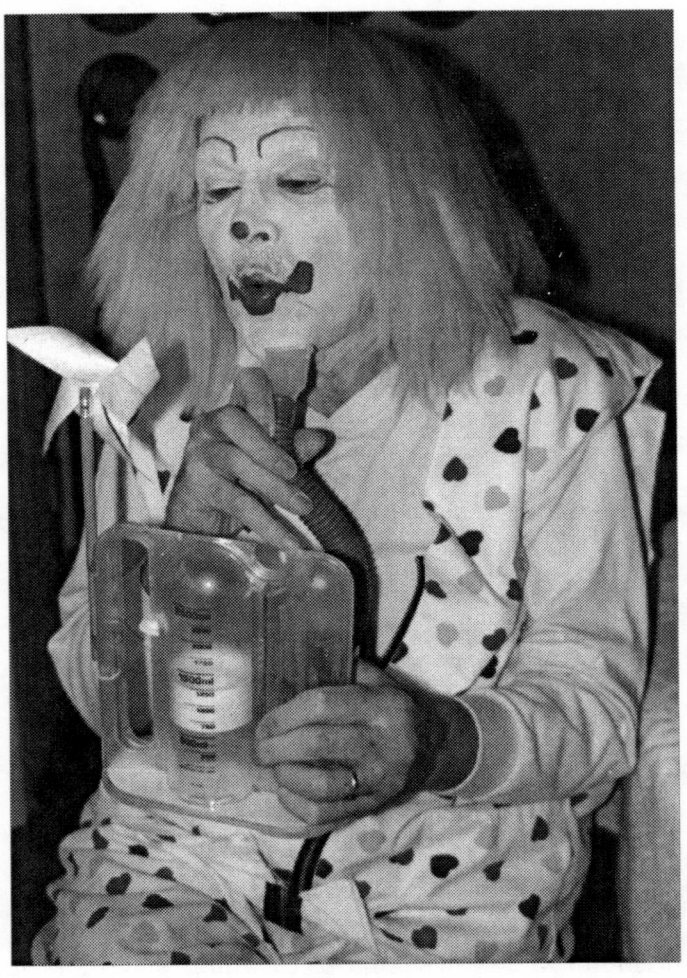

is called "Caring Clowns." We'll go more into our kind of "gig" later in the book.

Flawed Faces—Discovering Your Kind of Ministry

WHERE DOES CLOWNING BEGIN?

Our clown friend, Albert Alter, gave us a lasting picture of what makes a good clown. Albert had spent time as a trained Barnum and Bailey Circus clown. Albert was in a room with Lou Jacobs, one of their greatest circus clowns.

While he was in full clown someone asked Lou a question. "Lou, what makes a clown?"

Lou was an Auguste clown, which means everything is exaggerated. His head was extended by a wig and tiny hat. Makeup around the eyes and mouth enlarged them. Then there was his large-fashioned, bulbous red nose.

Lou pointed to his nose and said, "Not here," then pointed to his heart, "but here."

Once you accept that you have a flawed face, you can deal with the heart matter. That's where motivation, understanding, and all of our abilities to relate originate. Someone has suggested that we learn to "listen with the ears of our hearts." That's gaining insights that you observe from relating to others. Caring clowns know and observe this even with flawed faces.

All too often we think perfection is the means to a needful end. The faces of clowns, even those meticulously designed, are not perfect. Yet, with the personality of the clown at work, the face and costume are secondary. How and what you do with that relationship is what is important.

Bring in the Clowns—
A Metaphor for Ministry

In one of her earliest solo clowning experiences, Lenore went to a special outing for developmentally-challenged young adults. It was held in the parking lot of a Roman Catholic church that was centrally located. When she arrived, she was a bit overwhelmed. For a few moments she wondered if this was really the place to be.

Off to one side stood a gorgeous, well groomed, and meticulously-made-up clown. He just stood there like a statue to be observed. He didn't do anything. She supposed he was just wanting to be seen. He must have spent hours getting ready, and he looked beautiful. But he just stood there.

Wrinkles got caught up in the action of the youth. There was music playing, so she gently approached one of the youth. Together they danced and interacted with joyous delight. That interaction continued for about an hour with other youth. When it was time for her to leave, she was exhausted.

On the way to her car a reporter from a local newspaper stopped her. He had noticed what she had been actively doing. He asked her about the experience.

"Oh, I just saw these people out there and thought they might like to dance. So, I got started and we all had fun."

"But the other clown," he continued, "didn't do anything but just stand there."

Flawed Faces—Discovering Your Kind of Ministry

"Well, I guess he had different training than I had. Besides, I like people, and these young adults were a lot of fun for me as well."

When you feel flawed as a person, sometimes you try to cover it with actions, or maybe with grease paint. Instead of reaching out to others, you just stand there hoping someone will notice you. The emphasis is upon you and not the other person. The kind of clowning we learned from Floyd Shaffer and many others, made us consider others first. Then we respond in that moment where they are. From my reading of the Scriptures, I think Jesus often responded that way, thinking of others first.

Ministry can bring that experience as well. Our second child Martha was a pleasant little girl. By the time she was three, we discovered a major flaw inside her body. She had a cancerous Wilms tumor on one of her kidneys. At the time, it was considered 98 percent fatal.

How do you deal with ministering to your own child in a case like that? You feel so flawed yourself. You wonder if somehow you passed along a gene in which this cancer existed. In all reality, we didn't know and still don't more than forty years later.

In her last hospital stay, Martha was very concerned about her older sister. Members of the church I was serving at the time had sent many gifts to Martha in the hospital. Somehow, Martha sensed her older sister Margaret's envy of all the stuffed animals. At the time

Bring in the Clowns—
A Metaphor for Ministry

Margaret was just five, so a tiny bit of jealousy over the attention Martha received must have existed.

Late one afternoon, from her hospital bed Martha told Margaret, "You can have any of those animals that you want." I can't remember if or how many Margaret might have accepted. But here was a very flawed child whose life was just about over. Yet, she was able to be aware of her sister's feelings and sought to relieve any sense of jealousy.

In that same hospital, Martha often wanted to be taken by wheelchair to see an older woman. Somehow Martha sensed that this woman was alone and she just wanted to come and say hello. Out of her own need for comfort she was able to offer it to another. Martha wanted to comfort that "grandma."

No doubt those of you who read this can remember when you have had experiences similar to this. Someone took the time to share a moment or two with you. Your spirits were lifted, and you were not alone. You were understood and accepted.

Every Christmas and Easter we receive a lovely card for the occasion. It comes from a widow whom we have known for years. We seldom see her, but she never forgets us. Part of it was due to our experiences with her husband and family members. There continues to be this mutuality of shared experiences we had with her and her family. Her thoughtfulness touches us with each card.

Flawed Faces—Discovering Your Kind of Ministry

Her life changed dramatically at his death, and she had to carry on. She has done a marvelous job of moving

on. Memories continue, but life has a quality for her that says, "Keep moving, even though you are now alone."

Ministry is getting to know the floor on which you live, that place where there is an openness to "see." Once on that floor you can begin to fashion the kind of ministry that comes to you, even with your imperfections.

For Lenore and me, the serendipities that confront us are sometimes most difficult. Martha's illness and ultimate death were crucial and cut deeply into our psyches and faith.

I well remember sitting on Martha's bed at home while she was in the hospital. I had just spent several hours in the hospital with her. I could see life draining

Bring in the Clowns—
A Metaphor for Ministry

all too quickly out of her tiny body. In the midst of my fear and deep frustration I shouted out to God, "Look, I gave my life to you in ministry and you do this to me! How come?"

My bony right fist was thrust up in the air with a sense of utter futility. I didn't know it at the time, but that was when the good Lord gently grasped my hand and held it. He knew what it meant to have a Son die young.

Years later, as I've reflected on it, I realized that God does not reject us. God loves with an inexhaustible love. He grabs our shaking fists and opens them up, saying in effect, "Receive my love and carry on. I'll not leave you...ever."

So with flawed theology, "It's your fault, God, for taking my child," I still was called to carry on. Ministry wasn't for the moment or for a few years. "Ministry," as good friend Dennis Benson tells me, "never ends. You have to keep dropping breadcrumbs for others to find their way. Your calling doesn't end with retirement. Most likely it will continue long after you have died. That's your legacy to encourage others to discover their ministries as well. Our few 'crumbs' may bring encouragement to others to carry on."

It is because of people like Dennis, that many of us are doing our best to leave those bits and pieces. We discovered some of them ourselves from the many folks we have met who have shared their ministries with us.

Flawed Faces—Discovering Your Kind of Ministry

Whether or not you ever put makeup on your flawed face, let the idea of discovering your ministry take place. Perfection doesn't happen in this life. So move off your "floor," your starting place. Use the gifts you have and be open to serendipities of the spirit. It can be dicey at times and can come at great cost. We'll share a bit of that personally in later chapters.

In one of the churches I served, we had a number of people who were not typical leaders. They were honest, well-meaning elders and deacons, but felt shortchanged in leadership style. With a lot of coaching and using their willingness to serve, they became excellent leaders. They surprised themselves, the church, and even me. But the good Lord knew they could serve, and how willingly they did. Not typical middle-class leaders, but once on the job, they assumed their responsibilities and ran with them.

In the 1960s I was serving a small urban church. Of the 130 members, not more than a handful had any advanced education. Most were workers in factories, maintenance jobs, and the like. Very few were professionals. They were a totally different kind of congregation than what was considered Presbyterian at the time.

Yet, they were so ready to be open to try different things. Their flawed faces were only a means to do something else. With the help of a union musician, we offered the community a free concert. "Joy for Free" was its title. Jazz was the vehicle, and we received a grant from the local musicians union to pay the musicians that day.

Bring in the Clowns—
A Metaphor for Ministry

The sanctuary was filled with neighbors who happened inside the place for possibly the first time. Or they may have been there because it was also a polling place to vote.

Response to the event allowed us, a small urban congregation, to put on the face of wonder and joy, then give it away. It was surprising to many people in that congregation that they pulled it off. They were lifted off their floor of thinking they were too small and unimportant. God's gift of music warmed the hearts of people in the area that day. More on this experience later.

This was in those fairly charged days of the 1960s. Hippies and new music blasted out for free love plus some questionable actions. Yet it brought about the emphasis on men's hair. Should it be long or short? Then there were the beards and long sideburns.

I chanced a fairly safe trial of facial hair. My light beard never materialized in anything dramatic, so I ditched that. But sideburns were my choice. After they had done a good job of growing, I heard an interesting comment. One of the teenagers came up to me after worship one Sunday. David said, "Thanks, Mr. Bud, for having sideburns. You made them legal for me and other kids."

A year or so later we did a pastoral exchange with a congregation in Australia. I had become so accustomed to my facial hair I didn't think much about it. Yet, I needed to keep the sideburns on because my passport picture showed them. After a few months in Geelong, I made an interesting discovery. Some of the men there began growing "side-boards" as they were called.

Just before we left that exchange, the congregation gave us a going-away party. I had used many of the Peanuts cartoons in my sermons, so someone in the congregation drew a large picture. It was of Linus with huge "side-boards." Who says facial hair is flawed! Mine brought both humor and respect that I never realized.

QUESTIONS FOR REFLECTION:

1. What was the place or the occasion when you felt that ministry was your calling?

2. If you are currently in ministry as a professional or volunteer, where have the serendipities come to you? How did you respond? Where has the experience led you? How did you feel when you decided not to follow the leading at the moment? Did you later regret it? Or were you glad you discovered that it wasn't really meant for you? Were you able to discuss it with someone at the time? Did you find someone else who could follow it?

3. In how much of a "box" have you put ministry? Certain styles, non-threatening changes, or cop-outs?

Bring in the Clowns—
A Metaphor for Ministry

4. How do you handle challenges to leadership in ministry, yours or others, be they lay or professional?

5. When you are looking for leadership in the church, do you usually look for those who seem most eager to lead? What about those who are a bit more reluctant, but you think could do the job? How much time and effort do you make to include them rather than turning back to the "usuals"? How can you unearth them? What "eyes of your heart" are you using?

6. If you're into clowning, what kind of clowning have you discovered uses your gifts the most? Where has it led you? Where would you like it to go? What kinds of resistance have you discovered, not just in church, but in the community? How do you deal with rejection of you as a clown?

7. In what ways do you just "stand" without getting involved with others you don't know or who are different from you? How are you able to begin some movement? Is your reluctance a sign of shyness, or are you not wanting to "interrupt" others by your comments or questions? Are you afraid to get involved and possibly be misunderstood?

8. Look again at the twelve disciples whom Jesus chose. Be reminded that their flaws were accept-

able to Jesus. He certainly was able to use that motley crew. That's why we're here. Look again at those with whom you minister. Mirrors not only reveal flaws, but often reveal little nuances of joy like "crow's feet"—smile lines from the eyes. Take some time to scan your face, even if it means closing the bathroom door. Then do as our clown friend Shobi Dobi reminds us: "Make a funny face every time you pass a mirror." She means it whether "in face" or just your normal face. You might discover more humor than you anticipated.

We all know perfection doesn't happen in this life. So move off the "floor" with whatever flaws you have. God knows how to use us as we are and can become one day at a time.

Chapter 3

Colors On The Face—
More Than Games in
Clowning and Ministry

Once you decide what kind of clown you want to become, you have the choice of colors. It needs to be said here that "becoming" is a continuing process. That's true for clowning and ministry. You are on a constant learning curve.

When I became a tramp clown, black was one of the dominant colors. The beard is usually that color. Except if I grew one now, it would be white. Around the mouth I trace a large, sad, forlorn, upside-down mouth. This is done with a black eyeliner pencil. Clown white is added inside this "mouth." The beard area is done with black theater makeup. My cheeks have a little trace of very light red rouge. A little white is added near or under the eyes to highlight them. My eyebrows are dabbed with some of the black used for the beard.

Bring in the Clowns—
A Metaphor for Ministry

Either a red sponge nose or one professionally purchased is added and affixed with special latex glue. Friend Albert Alter says even rubber cement can be lightly used. We were reminded in one of the conferences on clowning we attended to also color your own nose red. That's in case some very smart-aleck person grabs and takes your sponge nose, you'd still be in costume.

One of the key clown makeup books is Strutter's *Complete Guide to Clown Makeup.* Jim Roberts, a.k.a. Strutter the Clown, has done a wonderful job describing clown makeup. Illustrations abound. It's available through Players Press, Inc. P.O. Box 1132, Studio City, CA 91614-0132. This would be an excellent book to share with those starting to clown. We have suggested to clowns we've trained that they purchase the book.

When you look at a tramp or hobo clown you can have a feeling of disgust or sympathy. Going back to my first solo experience in a Florida hotel is a reminder of these responses. Here I was in essentially some of my ordinary, though sloppy-looking clothes. A dumpy hat my wife wished I had lost on one of our trips topped my head. My face was white with an awful blue beard.

Floyd Shaffer sent us neophyte clowns out on a "plunge." That's what he called our first experience because we "plunged" into our character. Then we "plunged" into an unsuspecting public! I was given a few balloons and set out on my own. My place of first encounters was near the front desk of the hotel. I just stood there trying to blow up a balloon, but was deliberately having no success.

Just then an older couple who were also staying at the hotel saw me. They looked over my actions and for a scary moment I wondered what they would do or say.

The older woman turned to her husband and said, "Look at that poor clown. He can't blow up his balloon."

Surprisingly, I had a positive response. Quickly I gave her my balloon. As she and her husband worked on blowing it up, I moved to another part of the area. I pulled out another balloon and repeated the procedure. Clowning had hooked me, and little did I realize it would last for more than twenty-five years!

Ministry is like that, full of serendipities and awesome challenges. Ministry is more than a game of events or places. I saw this in a negative way early in my ministry. A conference was being held for those of us who were Ministers of Christian Education. These were wonderful places to share ideas and learn ways to be creative. But it was also an occasion when I wondered if this is what my calling was all about.

One of the other clergymen who was there talked about an open position with another church. He said something like, "Boy, that's a great 'cherry' to be picked!" Meaning, ministry was more about salary than about serving. Since I had a family with four children, that had to be a concern. But I didn't feel salary and benefits were the ultimate measure of my "calling."

Bring in the Clowns—
A Metaphor for Ministry

It was then that I understood more clearly what the white in the clown makeup represented. Floyd Shaffer reminded us that white has quite a different meaning in other cultures. Lenore, in her work with refugees from all over the world, learned that quickly.

"Some of the refugees from Africa have a different view. White to them is a sign of death. When they attend a funeral, they wear white. It is both a reminder of the person who has died and that we, too, will one day die. This is not a negative response. It is a recognition that we are mortal."

We remember this whenever we apply white to our faces. There may have been some issues between Lenore and me before the gig. Things like concern over the details of the gig, or did we arrive with all the materials we needed? Items like this can create tension in a relationship, especially when we want to be as perfect as possible. There is always tension to move beyond the floor of our basic feelings to those creative and supportive ones. Putting on the white reminds us of the need to be strong in our relationships. We don't want anything to cause them to diminish or die.

HOW THIS AFFECTS OUR
CLOWNING AND MINISTRY

Through the twenty-five years as clowns we have been called to lead services of worship. Our usual pattern is to transform from Lenore and Bud into Wrinkles and

Colors On The Face—More Than Games in Clowning and Ministry

Doolotz right before the congregation. The Scripture passage we use is from 2 Corinthians 5:16-20. We use a variety of translations, but always end up essentially with one phrase. "If anyone is in Christ, they are a new creation. Behold, the old is gone and the new has come."

We have transformed from our usual persona to "new" persons. In the process we use the story of the white to indicate the death of the old person.

Bring in the Clowns—
A Metaphor for Ministry

The symbolism is a reminder of our daily need to be transformed.

However, that's not the end of the process. Our dear teacher, Floyd Shaffer, reminded us to tell about the colors. The white is for death, but the colors we put on our faces remind us of resurrection. We are new persons in Christ. That we can celebrate. We are Easter people and Alleluia is our theme song.

When we are asked to share a clown service of worship, we always conclude the service with the giving of a small red dot. This is usually offered on the cheek or back of the hand. It's essentially what friend Floyd Shaffer calls "The Mark of the Clown," which is also the title of one of his defining clown books!

Over the years we have had a wide variety of responses to that dot! What it signifies to us is that as Christians, we are all marked with the love of Jesus our Lord. That's something to celebrate and to share. It can also be a means of identity beyond the church service.

One of the most memorable experiences happened when we were asked to help with a workshop at a conference for Compassionate Friends. If you are not acquainted with this organization, make a note to find out about it. Essentially, it is for parents who have experienced the death of a child.

That child may be stillborn or have other health problems, have had an accident, or be a victim of violence. Certainly, the loss of a son or daughter in war is another form of adult loss. With all the tragedies that fill the news, there is a great need for this organization.

Those who chose our little workshop wondered how clowning could have any place there. Like most of the other course leaders, we told our story about our daughter Martha, who had died of cancer. Then we began to weave that into our discussion with the people in the class.

It all led to us doing a "transformation" in front of them. At the conclusion, we gave them the mark of the clown. Only this time it became a symbol of their identity with others who had lost a child.

At the conclusion of the conference of several hundred people, we were asked to offer the red dot to anyone who wanted it. So Wrinkles and Doolotz stood at the doors of the conference hall. There we offered the dot to people as they left. Several days later we received a very moving story.

Participants in the weekend conference had dealt with many strong emotions. Some wanted to just go off to another place in Portland to privately "debrief" before returning to their homes.

One couple chose a waterfront park. There they could walk slowly or sit and look at the Willamette River. While they were sitting, another couple came by. They wore a red dot on their cheeks just like the couple sitting on the bench. Immediately they were caught up in very powerful emotions and shared their time together. Complete strangers found identity in one another.

Recently, we shared a nonverbal clown communion service with the congregation of Westminster Presbyterian Church where we worship. Details of the clown communion will be described later. However, the red dot on a cheek played another interesting story.

After worship one of the young women went to have coffee in a favorite café. She hadn't thought to wipe off the red dot. Possibly she just forgot it was there. But when she was served her coffee, the waitress asked about it.

Before long, this "marked" woman was sharing the experience of the Lord's Supper with the staff and some of the customers. The red dot, the Mark of the Clown, gave her an opportunity to witness for the Lord. Otherwise, she probably would have more naturally just carried on a light conversation.

Some persons who have received the red dot wipe it off before they leave the church. Isn't that how we sometimes think of our witnessing the faith? It becomes channeled to a building and a particular group of people. An ongoing experience we have had in clowning is that opportunities exist to share all the time. We often need some means to share it.

Colors On The Face—More Than Games in Clowning and Ministry

THESE "FACES" FOUND A SURPRISING OUTLET FOR MINISTRY

Dr. Franklin Woo and his wife Jean took a number of people to China on a Presbyterian Traveling Seminar. When we asked them if they had room for us, Frank said, "If you bring your clowns along!"

Frank had taken part in a short, half-day course in clown makeup. We were at the Presbyterian Stony Point Conference Center, in Stony Point, New York, for a year as mission volunteers. Classes had been set up and offered to people in the area. Frank, who lived in the area at the time showed up. He was able to only take part of one day, even though the course lasted several days.

He obviously enjoyed what he learned. With his keen intelligence and knowledge of Chinese culture, Frank felt that our clowns would be helpful. We'll explain more

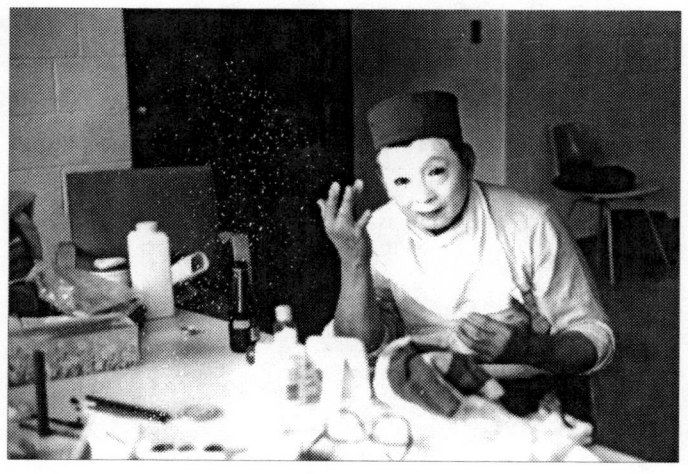

of the experience in another part of this book. But this has to do with that rather infamous red dot.

It happened in China at the Jiangshu Bible School. There we had been asked to share our clowning transformation experience. Mrs. Jean Woo gave a short introduction to the students in Chinese. Then, Lenore and Bud transformed into Wrinkles and Doolotz. Being nonverbal clowns was helpful. The room was full of young men and women in their 20s and 30s.

Some of our traveling seminar participants took digital pictures of our work. This helped us much later to evaluate the experience. But the red dots were an experience we had not anticipated.

We had done our little transformation during which Wrinkles gave Doolotz a red dot on his cheek. She already had them on her face during her transformation. They are part of her makeup.

The service also included a deeply moving experience of the death and resurrection of Christ. The music accompanying most of the service was from Jesus Christ Superstar, the crucifixion scene. Then the music segued to an instrumental version of the "Hallelujah Chorus" from The Messiah. A joyful mood was set because of the music.

This brought a "formal" conclusion of the service of worship. Now it was time for the mark of the clown, the red dot. Wrinkles and Doolotz left the chancel area and went down different aisles of the sanctuary. The joyful music continued.

At the end of each row we handed a student a cue-tip with a bit of washable red color on the tip. We marked the first person and then gave them the cue tip. Non-verbally, we signaled for them to mark their neighbor.

They followed instructions well and marked the next person. Then they passed the cue-tip to that person. The process was repeated down each row. Just about everyone in the room was marked. From the pictures we received later, the actions of the students were hilarious. They greatly enjoyed the experience of "marking" one another.

We then collected the cue tips and laid them on the Communion table. Silently we knelt for prayer. After we rose, Wrinkles and Doolotz gave each other hugs. Non-verbally we urged the students to do the same. The service was concluded with them greeting one another while we slipped out of the sanctuary. There was gentle pandemonium as the students overcame their customary dignity and offered hugs to each other.

Jean Woo then spoke to the congregation asking them, "Where were the clowns?" They were already there, for all were marked. That was perhaps the most joyous celebration of sharing the red dot, the witness of Christ's love, that we've experienced.

Colors in the context of worship can strengthen the bonds of commitment to Christ. Those colors don't have

Bring in the Clowns—
A Metaphor for Ministry

to be only on the robes or vestments of the clergy. They can become vehicles of communicating the gospel on the very faces of laypersons. Be that in a coffee shop with a young woman or a narrow side road in a Chinese city.

Ministry of hope and encouragement sometimes needs to have this colorful experience. The process of what happens becomes another serendipity of the Spirit. It's also an occasion on which to hang a memory.

CHANGING COLORS IN MINISTRY

In the fall of 1970 I discovered another shade of ministry. It was while I was serving on the Oregon Council of Churches Media Team. One of the members was a talk-show host for a program called Open Door. This was early radio talk-show programming. Essentially, it was a

Colors On The Face—More Than Games in Clowning and Ministry

question-and-answer format with a guest. The program was recorded several days ahead of time.

But now the host wanted to leave the program. After watching him manage a half-hour program, I thought it would be easy. So I jumped in, only to discover the need for a lot more preparation than I had anticipated.

The first few programs went along fairly well. But then a few of them were struggles, even after I had done research. The person I would be interviewing and I were in a studio. In the control room a DJ who had just gone off the air would check microphone levels. He'd start a tape recorder and throw a cue to begin. Once the interview began, the DJ left the control room to grab a cup of coffee. All I had was a stopwatch and a few notes.

We had 28:30, a minute and a half short of thirty minutes to do the interview. About half way through the interviews I would begin to get what we called "sweaty hands." There was no one in the control room, and if my guest was not too verbose, I could be in trouble.

After one taping, the program director of 62KGW, Hal Widsten called me into his office. Since I was just a volunteer, I knew I could be told that Open Door would be "closed." I supposed I could be "fired" if that was the case. However, Hal had another idea.

At the time, he had been working with students at Portland State University. They were putting together a program in their media department. Their dynamics were to include some of the contemporary music of the

67

day with poetry. Comments on political issues were also included. But since they were students, the process of continuing the program came to an end with each quarter.

Hal suggested I try this different approach. At the time, 62KGW was changing its format from a MOR (Middle of the Road) kind of music to rock. This meant I had to begin listening to the music that our teenage daughter had been playing on our Hi-Fi set at home. Not really the stuff for a man raised on Glenn Miller, Tommy Dorsey, and other big bands.

Margaret allowed me into her world of Chicago, Simon and Garfunkle, the Beatles, Bob Dylan, and others of that genre. Fortunately, there were lyric sheets

in the albums that allowed me to know what was being sung.

Then a new idea came about. Why not use the youth in the high school group at Kenilworth Presbyterian Church? Being the pastor, I already knew the youth and had been involved with some of their meetings. Kenilworth was a small urban church of roughly 130 members. Most of the parishioners and the area as well were people from working class employment. But they were willing to adjust and try new innovations.

So with the small group of about a dozen young people, we launched into a radio program. It would be a mix of poetry and short essays mixed with current music that somehow related to the readings. From the very beginning it was to be their program.

Thus, the voicing of the readings was and almost always included the same-age voices of those to whom it was aimed. Essentially I was to be the media midwife. The "stars" of the program were the youth and the listeners who provided writings from their "stage."

Interestingly, at about that same time, 62KGW rose in the ratings and finally became the number-one station in Portland. The rise had very little to do with our program, but we rode the wave of the station's popularity. We were grateful for the ride.

Open Door at that time was airing at 10:00 am on Sundays. Three other public affairs programs aired before us. Open Door signed off with "Day by Day," music

Bring in the Clowns—
A Metaphor for Ministry

from Godspell. Following a station ID, Casey Kassem's "America's Top 40" syndicated program came on.

62KGW was now the number-one station in Portland, and Open Door had the highest rating of any public affairs program. A sizable audience had become our listeners.

It needs to be said that our goal was not a "religious" program with constant calls for commitment to Christ. That would have been inappropriate to "color" our program that way. Rather, it was what I called "pre-evangelism." We gently challenged listeners to consider God as a live option in their lives.

UNHINGED? Listen to OPEN DOOR

MUSIC & COMMENTS BY YOUNG ADULTS

Over the years we had many persons who accepted that challenge. We weren't in the business of keeping numbers of converts. But through the years many became committed persons, active in their newfound faith in Jesus. They wrote to tell us of their decisions. We were thrilled to learn of their response.

For the next twenty-one years, Open Door expanded from one station to being aired on nearly 100 rock'n roll, contemporary stations around the country. It reached out through more than 400 stations and outlets of the Armed Forces Radio service around the world. A short-wave station, HCJB in Quito, Ecuador, carried the program into Iron Curtain countries, Asia, Africa, and even the Soviet Union. Another shortwave station aired us in the Philippines.

Listeners from all over the world sent in their prose and comments. It was my task to integrate them into the program. For the first several years I would write one weekly 30-minute program. Several of the teenagers would write the next two. However, this became a problem for them as they also had schoolwork to accomplish.

I had to make adjustments with pastoral duties as well. The radio program required that I take time to listen to music. Also, I needed to go through the prose and ideas that were sent to us by listeners. My pastoral day lengthened. Much of the selection and organizing the program came after regular pastoral hours. That meant evenings.

The youth made many suggestions of music and writings. Difficult subjects were raised along with the music that accompanied the times. The Viet Nam War was a concern. War, peace, environment, and teenage pregnancy were among their age-group concerns. Sexual child abuse was a topic Open Door dug deeply into long before it became a major topic in the rest of the media.

Bring in the Clowns—
A Metaphor for Ministry

One young girl heard one of our programs on abuse and wrote that her stepfather had abused her. She had asked for a copy of the fully-scripted program we had produced for the program. In my correspondence with her I asked if she had ever written down her thoughts. Shortly afterward she sent some very stinging prose that one of our youth interpreted for another program on the subject.

It was a very potent program that was recognized not only by our listeners, but by national media. "Abuse" was one of more than forty programs Open Door produced to receive a national media award.

An earlier program received the prestigious George Foster Peabody Award, considered the highest in broadcasting. The title of that program was simply "Insanity" that dealt with the Viet Nam war and erratic things happening in Portland at the time. Most of that 30-minute program had been put together by two teenagers.

BECOMING ADAPTIVE IN COLORING MINISTRY

Talk about changing one's "tune" and color in ministry. This was a turnaround experience for me. I had to return to the very ground floor of my understanding of theology. Along with that was the need to be an open listener to what teens were saying and music to which they resonated. I had to be stretched.

In the process I was able to observe many surprising places where faith was to be found. Many letters from listeners revealed their desire to learn more about faith and particularly about Jesus.

In some cases it was difficult for me to respond face-to-face. They lived in other parts of the country. So I would send copies of letters received from listeners to pastors in the cities from which they came. My deepest regret was those pastors who didn't know what to do with the letters or how to make contact, even when given the name and address of the listener.

A good friend in the church I was then serving was a super salesman by profession. Bob said, "If I had hot leads like that, I'd be on them right away." Perhaps the church needs to have that kind of lively color for outreach!

Like the varying colors of makeup on the face of my clowns, I had to be adaptive. But at the same time I found new depths of insights that my teenagers found in their music. I was surprised to find subtle hints of Scripture in music by artists who may not even know their source.

This was a time of real "message" pop music. With the listeners' prose, I tried to interpret that message. This was an opportunity that opened up my sense of grace. Dr. Paul Tillich once described grace as acceptance. He urged people to "accept the fact that God has accepted you." Then you can move on. You don't have to prove to God that you are lovable.

Bring in the Clowns—
A Metaphor for Ministry

The coming of Jesus revealed for all time what God thinks about his creations. We are deeply and profoundly cared for by the God Jesus revealed. Strangely, I found that some rock music spoke that same language.

Early in Open Door's development, I was called to serve a struggling suburban church. When I answered the calling, I asked if it was all right to continue with Open Door. They agreed. So some of the former youth in the Portland church joined in working on Open Door with suburban youth.

It was at Sunset Presbyterian Church that the clowning experience began. That service was described earlier. Together with the radio program and with a wife willing to discover the clown in her, the shadings of ministry changed. However, the sense of call remained for me to be true to my calling in Christ to serve him and encourage others.

Clowning and the Open Door radio ministry taught me one of the most endearing lessons in ministry. It continues to color my life even in retirement years. Listeners shared their precious and often very personal prose.

Somehow, though they did not know me personally, they trusted a complete stranger with their deepest thoughts. Then they allowed Open Door to share them with thousands of other listeners, some of whom were people who knew them. That could be scary for teens to reveal their inner thoughts by this means.

Colors On The Face—More Than Games in Clowning and Ministry

The lesson I learned from this was simply to begin with people where they are. So much religiosity wants to tell people where they need to be. In the process, all that is seen is one's own "colors," one's own opinions and beliefs. The tendency is to put people in that same mold.

God begins with you and me where we are. It's a reminder of that old wag that says, "Remember you're unique—like everyone else!" Indeed we are different colors, not just of skin, but of temperament and outlook. To put people into neat little categories usually is to have them feel "put off" for not hearing or seeing them for who they are.

Basic to our caring kind of clowning is to be "listeners," whether it is one person or many. What do you see and sense as you share your talents? The colors on your face and costume give you permission into some tender places. Rather than rushing into the face of a child, you stay your distance. After all, a clown in full face and costume is grotesque to a preschooler. You look like a monster. As clowns you need to be sensitive.

This sometimes leads to unique opportunities. Lenore had been clowning just for a short while. In a Sunday service at Sunset Church, she and several other clowns had been involved. It had been "Mission Sunday" and they had been used to highlight the theme. So she was in "full face" and costume by the end of the service.

Bring in the Clowns—
A Metaphor for Ministry

However, our daughter Margaret was flying in from some distant place shortly after the service of worship. We wanted to be there. Lenore, as Wrinkles, didn't have time to change makeup and clothes. So off we went to the airport. I was straight and she was a clown.

Once at the airport we started for the ramp where Margaret was to deplane. That was a time when you could do this. But in the meantime we had to go through the ticketing areas. Rather than going alongside of Wrinkles, I stayed a few paces back. The reason was to allow Wrinkles to clown her way to the plane. I was her silent support and protection.

This is basic when you are "in clown." You are "on" from the moment you are seen leaving home until you return. It can be wearing physically as well as emotionally to be "up" all this time. People wave to you in passing cars or on the streets. If you are driving, care is essential to maintain the fact that driving is your first and major response.

But here we were at the airport. One of the first persons we saw was a tiny preschooler who hadn't as yet seen the clown. The little girl was close to her parents when she first saw Wrinkles. She was startled. It may have been the first time she'd ever seen a clown. She grabbed her father's pant leg, but then peeked around the other leg at Wrinkles.

Remembering Floyd's teaching about space, Wrinkles kept her distance from the child, but all the time had eye contact. When the child squatted down, Wrinkles did the same. They were about thirty feet apart. The child could easily bounce up from her squatting position. Wrinkles had a problem and simply sat down, clown style, still keeping eye contact.

The child smiled ever so briefly. But she had had a non-threatening experience with a clown. She had been "colored" by a positive experience that would affect her outlook on more than clowns. Perhaps she learned that some strange people were "safe" and could be trusted.

When we came to the ramp where Margaret was to exit, Wrinkles met more challenges. She found an older couple waiting for a passenger to disembark from the same plane. In the process she caught the eye of the husband and did some coy things.

She took her colorful duster and dusted off his shoulders and sleeves. Then, because she sensed his openness, she offered this complete stranger a clown hug.

After Wrinkles had given him a good hug, he said to her, in his wife's hearing, "That's the best hug I've had in a long, long time!"

We hoped that episode didn't create any problems in that family. Maybe it opened up a whole new opportunity for dialogue between the husband and wife.

Shortly afterward our daughter came up the runway and saw her mother. She shouted loudly for all to hear, "This is my Mom!" and went quickly over to hug Wrinkles.

Bring in the Clowns— A Metaphor for Ministry

COLORING THE COMMUNITY AS WELL

Serendipities occur because they are not what you are expecting. In clowning and in ministry of all kinds, we need to have that awareness. God's loving Spirit may show up anywhere and in all kinds of guises. With a wee bit of imagination, new doors of opportunity come to color your ministry.

This happened again to us. We were in the process of wanting to have our house repainted. A good friend Bev Taylor had come over and we talked about colors. Since Oregon has many gray days, Bev suggested something with a little brightness. Together we decided on yellow with white trim.

From articles we'd read, we needed to check out exactly what tint that color should be. At a local paint store our minds were a bit boggled by all the shades and hues of yellow. But we decided on comparing about half a dozen. Finally asking for one called "Black Eyed Susan Yellow."

Helpful-hint articles suggested that we buy a small container and paint a few places on the house. We did this on our house. One spot would be shaded. Another in the bright sunlight. The appearance was rather interesting. Yellow and white areas of the house were seen from the streets around us. You couldn't miss them. They looked ugly with those splotches of brightness.

Then we waited to allow ourselves time to adjust to those colors. A neighbor friend came over and asked if that's the color we were going to paint. "It's pretty bright," was her remark.

Well, OK, so it is bright. At about this time we also had a community block party committee meeting at our house. I had gone down to the paint shop again and chose samples of softer yellow hues. With scotch tape I hung them on the backside of the house, one under another. They were taped on top of the bright yellow so the changes could be seen. They hung on a wall in our backyard adjacent to our deck. That way the colors couldn't have been seen from the street by committee members as they arrived for the meeting.

One by one, as the committee members came to the meeting, we took them out onto our deck. There we asked them to look at the new hues and tell us which one they liked. Most interestingly, out of five different shades of yellow they all chose the same one. So did we.

The block party committee was something I had worked on for the last two years. The year before had been quite successful, so we were planning again. Since we have only a few children in the area, as neighbors we don't seem to associate much together. We could say "hi" as we drove past someone and wonder who they were or where they lived.

Some of us wanted a little bit more, so the block party came about. We, as mostly adults in the area, could at least now say hello and have a little knowledge of who the people were and where they lived.

Bring in the Clowns—
A Metaphor for Ministry

From our experience with asking the committee members about the color of our house that they would be seeing, a little more community spirit was created. It is easy to lose that neighborly relationship by staying inside our own houses. Having them help us choose the color for our house gave us more of a sense of relatedness.

Isn't that part of what ministry is all about? We establish relationships that are more than surface. One neighbor, who wasn't part of the committee, rang our doorbell several days later. She had been talking to some of those who had helped choose our house's color. She wanted to have a voice in it as well.

Her house sits across the street and opposite one side of ours. From her house she would be looking at the most densely colored part of our house. It's a long wall with only two small windows. That view would be out her living room window. Thus, she had been concerned about the brightness as well. The early morning sun would have bounced off our east wall right into her west-facing living room.

Most interestingly, without telling her which color others had voted as favorite, she chose the same one. By this time, about ten people in our community had a part in choosing the color of our house. Now they had a personal investment in our house and the neighborhood. Maybe we should have suggested that they help pay for the house painters!

Colors On The Face—More Than Games in Clowning and Ministry

Colors and community do have relatedness. The color of a house, a new car, or the faces of clowns cause us to consider how we relate to them. For clowns and ministry, there are many hues from which to choose.

Check out what kinds of colors your pastor wears on Sunday, in a stole, a bright tie or a stunning dress. Color does affect our ministries.

Just a reminder that if you are open to begin where people are, those opportunities afford themselves. Often it happens more times than we're willing to accept. Let them color your ministry with encouragement and hope.

QUESTIONS TO CONSIDER

1. Where have you discovered new "colors" in your ministry? What places and persons influenced you unexpectedly?

2. Who have been persons who have given encouragement to you when you felt down? Have you been lifted by someone whose life may be physically or emotionally challenged? Have those experiences challenged your faith?

3. How do you respond to persons who are different from you in language, ethnicity, education, and levels of experience? How have you dealt with challenges to your ministry, often by people who obviously don't want any answer?

Bring in the Clowns—
A Metaphor for Ministry

4. Where have you been able to be used in ways you never thought were open to you? How do new ideas of Scripture test your faith? How about those of differing faith communities? Are there parts of their expressions of faith that you find amenable to your faith, too? What does that do to your understanding of relating to your Creator?

5. How do you deal with "games" in ministry, some you create and some who play their "tricks" on you? Things like political and theological paradoxes that have no one solid answer, but someone is asking you to make it either true or false?

6. In what place does grace, aka "acceptance," find a place in the way you color your ministry?

7. If you could name a color for how you look at your ministry what would that color be?

Chapter 4

Clothing the Clown—
Where Ministry Takes You

The next step in the process of becoming a clown is how to clothe that clown. This will also be the means by which you gain entry into the various arenas where you share your gifts. In many ways, this is also a call to creativity in ministry.

It's important to remember that being a clown is a gift. So is ministry. These gifts don't just happen. There is a sense of rightness in your psyche that says "OK" to this new venture. Eventually, you will learn great gratitude in being led to clowning and ministry.

Without a sense of gratitude neither of them will be significant to you or to your Maker. Often you will exclaim, "My God, thank you for allowing me to be a part of this." This holds true in both clowning and ministry which only doubles when it involves both.

Bring in the Clowns—
A Metaphor for Ministry

Remember that both clowning and ministry may be done by volunteers. Having a thoughtful and professional sensitivity is what matters.

WHERE THAT GIFT FIRST REVEALED ITSELF

Having the opportunity to interview a former clown was my beginning. We called the radio program, would you believe, "Clowning"? In actuality, the program became the subtle awareness of another gift that needed to be unearthed. That program for the Open Door radio program led me to a media conference in Florida. To our surprise, it had won the Gabriel award from UNDA-USA, the Roman Catholic media organization.

And there I met Floyd Shaffer.

The gift of clowning was very simple, even though I hardly knew what I had been given. Any present that is meant to be shared needs time to be evaluated and nurtured. I found this true when I initially felt the awesome challenge to professional ministry.

Where I realized this calling was hardly a pastoral setting. I had been dating a young college student for several months. Both of us attended Oregon State College. (That's what it was called at the time; now it's a university.) Following a date we were sitting in my little 1937 Plymouth coupe outside her home in Portland. We were talking about a lot of things, mostly school and us.

Clothing the Clown—
Where Ministry Takes You

Somewhere in my conversations with Jackie, I sensed a couple of things. One was that she and I would only be good friends. The other deep feeling was a calling, for lack of another good word, to continue my education and enter seminary.

Now I can't say this was the first experience of that calling. It just became stronger at that time than I could express. From memories that go back over fifty years, all I can remember is that the setting was almost unreal. It was the most illogical of places. I was on a date with a young woman for whom I was really fond and in front of her home in Portland. Not a mountain-top experience in the usual way, but a preparation to "clothe" me with seminary education.

Bells didn't ring. Wild lights did not shine. In fact, the strongest memory I have of the occasion was where it occurred. Right in front of her parents' house. Tall, stately fir trees were silhouetted against the evening sky. But it was the place where I began to clothe myself in a totally different lifestyle from what I had expected.

My time on the floor in the Galt Ocean Mile Hotel in Ft. Lauderdale, Florida, is also a reminder. Bells and whistles didn't occur there either. Just a cold, hard hotel floor accompanied by the gentle voice of Floyd Shaffer.

"This is where you begin, Bud. Get in touch with what the Spirit is telling you. That's why you're here."

Pivotal moments in your life seldom come in exhilarating experiences. Most occur in the mundane and ordinary circumstances in which you find yourself. In fact, like me, you don't even know it. But those are just beginning places. Discovering the floor, the flawed faces, and colors are all openings for the Spirit to work.

Now there was the clothing of that experience.

FINDING THE CLOTHING, LITERALLY

For my Doolotz clown, I simply went to a local Goodwill Industries store. Incredibly, I found the basics of my outfit. An old black sport coat and a pair of bright orange-colored polyester bell-bottomed pants right out of the 1960s. Also, a strange gray cloth aviator's helmet like those in WWI. But I needed something more.

I looked all around for some old-fashioned aviator's goggles, the ones you think of when the Red Baron's name is called. They are elliptical with a black elastic band to hold them on the face. Some cushioning material would be around the goggles. That way they could fit snugly on the face and also keep the wind out of the sides of the goggles in those open cockpits of Flying Jenny airplanes. There was only one place to find those goggles, an Army surplus store.

After going through many baskets and bins of old surplus stuff, I found what I was looking for. They were the only pair in the store. Sometimes the movement of the Spirit is found in the mundane places and times. This was one of them. To top it off, these goggles also had tinted glass. Terrific.

Clothing the Clown—
Where Ministry Takes You

Picture how bizarre the costume became. A tramp face, bell-bottomed polyester, orange-red trousers, black sport coat, and now an aviator's cap with dark goggles. I painted some old Nike tennis shoes red and yellow with leftover paint my sons had used to cover nicks in their bicycles.

Over the years Wrinkles and Doolotz have had many good experiences in our simple gigs using the aviator glasses. In most of our presentations in churches, schools, or wherever, we are silent, nonverbal clowns. That allows us to be in touch with ourselves and to know again and again that we are the audience. The people out beyond us are on the stage, and it is to them that we respond. More on that later.

So during a gig, right after we have completed our transformation, we let the audience know we've finished clothing our clown by bowing to them. Most of the time Lenore has finished earlier than I did. That's because I stay "straight" and do a little talk while she is transforming.

I explain to the people what the colors mean, and in church settings their faith significance. I also explain why we powder and splash water on our faces. It's not often you see a clown get "into face." Once I sit down to put on my face I go silent.

In the meantime, Wrinkles finishes her transformation. She silently addresses those present by bowing to them. She then goes out into where the people are, be

Bring in the Clowns— A Metaphor for Ministry

it a church congregation, a school, or Alzheimer's unit. She gives them attention by gently dusting them off with her colorful feather duster. She may sit on people's laps with their permission. This is to keep them occupied while I make my nonverbal transformation.

In most gigs we take about ten minutes to quickly put on our makeup, and another five minutes to get into our costumes. That's at least half the usual time to just do our faces when not in front of people! It's a quick job, but the symbolism is more important than being perfect.

The last movement I make after I'm clothed and in full face is to put on those dark-colored goggles. They appear darker than they are, but I act a little confused. I turn in the opposite direction from where people are sitting and bow.

Wrinkles quickly leaves what she is doing and comes to me. She wants to correct my direction. She turns me around toward where the people are sitting. Then to make Doolotz understand the reason for the change, she helps Doolotz remove the glasses. Then Doolotz can see the correct way to face. A gracious bow follows.

This may seem like a lot of attention to a little action, but this is a simple means of testing the audience. They don't know that they are the ones on stage. Yet, they will let you know whether or not you struck their funny bones. It will help you with your gig wherever it may occur.

Clothing the Clown—
Where Ministry Takes You

BEING IN THE MOMENT

Neither of us has taken an improvisational acting course. But we have learned the importance of "being in the moment" with people. That can be in a group of several hundred or a single, smiling wheelchair-bound person in a convalescent center.

Your colorful face and strange clothing can often give you permission to move into another's space. That space is both very private and very awesome. Not all your contacts will do this for you, but you'll learn quickly by eye contact if you are welcomed or rejected. More on how "space" is important a little later.

Once clothed and in "full face," you will be noticed! But, of course, that is what you want. Now you must respond to what you sense from others. This is "learning the joy of being fully in one place." [a phrase I read in PCUSA news release about a woman working with low-income people in Wapiti, Washington - check PCUSA news 4-22-05]

LEARNING WHO IS THE AUDIENCE
AND WHERE IS THE STAGE

One of the earliest learnings that came from clowning was to determine who is in control in a given situation. With our type of caring clowning, we've learned who is the audience and who is on stage. It's not what you think. Your outfit and makeup seem to mean, "I'm on stage." But it's really not that way for caring clowns.

Bring in the Clowns— A Metaphor for Ministry

You become the audience and the group or individual is on stage. This is deeply true of our clowning in hospitals. If you've been hospitalized, you know that doctors, nurses, aides, and even those doing housekeeping duties have more control than you do.

But to the caring clown, the person in the hospital bed is in charge. We gently ask if we can enter their "home," which is their room. Often doing this is by a simple, nonverbal gesture. They are the ones in charge. We give them the power to say no or yes. If yes, we can offer our simple, usually funny gig.

Then Mary Ann Harty's line becomes a reality: "Mirroring what the other person is feeling is the mark of the clown." In some settings that is actually what we do. A couple sitting in the surgery waiting area of the hospital, legs crossed and arms folded over their chests. If I sense in their eyes that I'm welcome, then I may sit down and fold my arms over my chest, simply mimicking them, all the time checking to see if I've gone too far.

Most times there is a smile or tiny giggle. The experience is over in a few moments. Their smiles are the pay. A moment of quiet endorphin release of tension is experienced by the person. Often a "Thank you, I needed that" comes from their lips. Talk about great "pay" for a volunteer assignment in a hospital. We have huge bank accounts filled with that kind of pay from our clowning.

Clothing the Clown—
Where Ministry Takes You

A slight momentary thought: if you are clowning, make sure you keep a log of what you've done. Do it right after you are finished before you lose track of what happened. When doing pastoral calling, I always carried some 3x5 cards to make notations as reminders. With all the new electronic gizmos, that can be even easier. However it is done, you will find that it will pay dividends for memory recall and also for personal encouragement.

THIS "CLOTHING" EFFECTS MINISTRY

All too often, we pastors feel like we are the "main show." I know it from personal experience! You get to feeling that you are the reason people attend a particular church. That's a real concern for all of us who feel called to professional ministry. We need some perspective.

There's an apocryphal story of a little old woman who was waiting outside a large church. She was a bit early before the service of worship, and the senior pastor came by. He asked her if she had a question.

"Yes," she said, "which of the pastors is preaching today?"

"Why, I am," said the senior pastor.

"Well, thank you," she replied. "I'll come again another time."

Most clergy I know are sensitive to the meaning of who is in charge of their ministry. This is not just a matter of a governing body, but an awareness of their congregation's needs. Sometimes that spills over into the clergy's own needs.

After spending time with a couple who had been experiencing some marital problems, the wife asked me how she could "repay" me for my counseling. She knew that my regular stipend was fine, but she wondered about something else.

I had been uncomfortable with some of the new ways of expressing thanks. Was there something in my psyche that kept me from showing a little more feeling toward a parishioner, male or female? Handshakes were fine most of the time, but something more seemed needed.

So I turned to Sarah and said, "Sarah, teach me how to hug as a clergyman."

With that, Sarah simply slipped her left arm inside my right arm and gave me a squeeze. No worries as a man hugging a woman for frontal hugs. But a simple acknowledgment that more than a handshake sometimes was appropriate for anyone. Over the years, I've found it to be one of the most gracious experiences to receive as well as give. How neat it is to see men hugging men out of respect and appreciation for their gifts.

LEARNING WHO IS CENTRAL

When we learn to share the load with other members, the situation can change. As we allow them to make their contribution, then we learn the lesson of the clowns. We clergy are the audience. The congregations we serve are the ones "on stage." They are the live ones from whom we learn and respond.

In the first church I served in rural Kansas, I was taught a wonderful, but hard lesson. I felt fairly confident. I'd had two years in the Army with some of it in combat. That seemed to age me well.

Add the fact that I was fresh out of four years of college with a Bachelor's Degree in Education, plus another four at San Francisco Theological Seminary where I earned two more degrees. I was twenty-eight years old, had a wife and brand-new baby daughter, with another child on the way. So I was feeling pretty potent.

Like many preachers, we become a bit protective of what we say in our sermons. They are reflections of our life experiences and hopes for the future, biblical truths that we feel need to be shared. Having the benefit of the most recent theological insights of anyone in that small rural Kansas congregation, I must have begun to "lord it over them." However, I had been pretty dense.

Two comments cleared it up for me within the first year. Our second child, Martha, was born, and my mother had come to assist Lenore with the children. She had heard me preach on a couple of Sundays. She stood by the sink preparing vegetables for the evening meal one Sunday.

I asked her, patronizingly I'm sure, what she thought of the services of worship. Of course, I was really asking about the sermons. From her 5' 1" height, she turned and almost looked eye to eye at my nearly six feet.

Bring in the Clowns—
A Metaphor for Ministry

"Bud," she said, "You gave 'em hell again this Sunday."

Wow! She may have been diminutive in physical stature, but she delivered a near knockout punch. That short mental jab is still felt. It is a reminder that I came in not knowing who was the audience. I wanted the stage. I wanted to be the shining star to my mother and the congregation.

That experience was coupled with the comments of one of the dear farmers a short time later. C. E. McKee, Jr., was clerk of the Session at the Federated Church in Spearville, KS. He was a college graduate and not afraid to help a young clergyman. I was paying a pastoral visit to his farm just east of Spearville.

C. E. and I were into a conversation about ensilage and how it works for cattle's feed. It needed time to "nurture itself and cure" before C. E. would feed it to his herd of cattle. Since it was late winter, steam rose from the carefully-placed ditch in which the ensilage was placed.

A little more personal steam was coming. At one point in the conversation I realized I was the audience. Almost repeating what my mother had observed earlier, C.E. said words that speak to me today.

"Bud, you don't have to tell us how bad we are. We already know that. Help us to become better."

How gracious C. E. McKee was to soften the spirit of a somewhat brazen young clergyman. Those words carried me long into my ministry whether in the pulpit, on the radio, or as a clown. Most effectively, I hope, in the ways in which I continued my ministry.

It is so easy to criticize from the supposedly "pole of superiority." But how humbling it is when gentle words are spoken to bring us to equal standings before the face of God. My mother and C. E. McKee, Jr. helped fashion my ministry very early. They were lessons that shaped how I clothed that ministry for the next forty-five years.

WHERE DO YOUR CLOTHES LEAD YOU?

I read that Dr. Albert Einstein felt that "imagination was more important than knowledge." It was nearly echoed by an editorial writer of the *New York Times* who said that we need to encourage more creativity in our classrooms and colleges. That certainly is the case with clowning, and I found it true in ministry as well. But one needs to be careful how far one goes with it.

In the early 1970s, I believe, one of the large corporations invented the word "imagineering" for their staff meetings. Since the word came through one of the employees who was a member of Kenilworth Church in Portland, Oregon, we used it a lot.

It became a catchphrase for us, but it also was a means of making our Session meetings more meaningful. Our committees did the same thing. We wanted to reach out to our community. Kenilworth area was very urban and barely touching on lower middle class for the most part.

One of our older members had a young single man whom she boarded. He worked at a liquor store for regular employment, but on the side was a musician. He had a gift with the upright bass and played with a combo in local bars at night.

Several of us from a special committee in the church grabbed onto that "imagineering" idea. We talked about a musical outreach into our community. Bob was asked for some input. He said, "Why don't we have a free jazz concert for the community? I know a number of musicians, and I think we can get a grant from the union to pay for the gig."

That began our first "Joy for Free" concert. Bob located the musicians. With his help, the church worked out an agreement with the union and signed the necessary papers. Then we began the publicity. Our youth were involved in distributing flyers within the few blocks of the neighborhood.

We made contact with both the community and city newspapers to announce "Joy for Free." It was to be a concert by local jazz musicians, and there would be no cost to those attending. We'd also have light refreshments afterwards.

A small women's singing group also made themselves available for the afternoon. So we had vocal as well as instrumental joy expressed.

Clothing the Clown—
Where Ministry Takes You

A specially-designed bulletin was prepared. This included using members of the church from various age groups. They read prose appropriate to their age group. The jazz combo or women's group played or sang music that added to the writing's thoughts. A copy of that service is in the Addendum.

The response from the community was great. Both members of the church and the community filled sanctuary seats. Joy certainly filled the sanctuary with some of the jazz tunes coming straight from Duke Ellington's spiritual music. Gospel and pop songs rattled the chimes next to the organ. But joy did abound that Sunday afternoon. It proved to be an effective outreach to the community.

Did it bring in new members? Not many as I recall. But people in the community were more aware of the church and had actually found out the walls didn't tumble in on them for being there! Fact is, we had a series of annual "Joy for Free" events. They included a small traveling theater group who did "Waiting for Godot," as well as a lovely Irish harpist, all giving their gifts to our part of the community. This whole process grew out of doing some "imagineering" about the clothes of ministry in our community.

CLOTHES OF A MUSICAL KIND

Personal "imagineering" certainly came into my ministry as I began to grapple with emerging rock'n roll

Bring in the Clowns— A Metaphor for Ministry

music. I found myself having to listen to many lyrics for the Open Door radio program. When I read the lyrics, I had a better understanding of what was being sung.

I needed to know the words before I could use the music. This was especially difficult, because I had grown up with lyrics that were easy to learn. They were clear and without too many little nuances.

About this time, a controversial record album was being foisted on the community. It was a rock opera called "Jesus Christ Superstar." Along with its release came controversy from and within churches. My time with Open Door was pretty new, but it opened an opportunity.

Hal Widsten, the program director for 62KGW where we recorded our program, had an idea. By now I was fairly comfortable being at the station, so he felt I might help him. He wanted to be the first station in Portland to air the complete album. Would I help?

He managed to get a number of complementary albums of the music from Decca Records. Now could I round up a number of clergy of different denominations? If they would be willing to come to the station and listen to the record, he'd give them a free album as a thank you.

Most clergy whom I asked were willing to spend an hour and half at the station listening to the music. Many people have some kind of mystical view of media places, so the intrigues of "place" as well as a free gift were enough to fill a conference room. It was another case of "imagineering."

To help set up the room before they arrived, I posted as many pictures of Jesus Christ that I could find. This was a simple visual device to set them at ease to think of Jesus in a slightly different way. As I recall, I had pictures of Jesus in some other ethnic settings than the usual ones. One I well remember was a Japanese rendition of Jesus.

When we were all settled in place, I introduced Hal. With little fanfare, Hal gave them the albums and told the pastors to follow the enclosed lyric sheets. He also asked them not to judge the album solely on its rock music, but look at the lyrics as well.

The music began. I'm not sure if I had heard the music ahead of time, but I watched these men; yes, that's who I had invited! The clergy gender gap was only beginning to open at that time. I didn't know any women pastors at that time.

Instead of controversy in the rock opera, those present were genuinely interested. They asked many questions and raised concerns especially since the rock opera only suggested the resurrection. What they had in their hands was a means of communicating with the youth and young adults of that day. An evolving revolution was taking place in music and they were in at an early starting point.

Bring in the Clowns—
A Metaphor for Ministry

Hal had a second plan. Would I like to be a part of a team to respond to the airing of the whole album on the following Sunday night? My only response was that I knew a couple of pastors who would enjoy and be good at responding to listeners' comments or questions. The pastors all had lyric sheets and were hearing the album for the first time themselves. I came to watch what happened.

From about 9:00 to 11:30 that Sunday night, "Jesus Christ Superstar" was on the air along with discussions. This was a very early listener-talk-radio style that was "live." I remember how "warm" the studio was with the several people of differing theological views sitting there listening. Then they gave their opinions of what they heard. Calls came flooding into the studio.

I'd like to have the audience numbers from that night at 62KGW. The great imagination of Tim Rice and Andrew Lloyd Webber helped spark a contemporary theological revolution. Somehow I had slipped into its clothing. It was part of the education of a small-church pastor in "the ways of the music world." This affected me for the next twenty years.

Somehow, it still manages to give me glimpses of God's imagining hands at work. As I type these words, some of the instrumental music of those days is playing. Maybe I only think I'm living in this moment.

Clothing the Clown—
Where Ministry Takes You

How the "clothes" we choose
affect our ministry

What we wear in our lives, both the actual clothing of choice and the bent of our minds, affect our ministries. A tramp clown elicits a sense of sadness and empathy. The ecclesiastical garments of a new pope declare the majesty of the role he is serving. You feel what you wear. Or as one of the garment manufacturer's commercial states, "I guarantee it."

The same is true of our sensations regarding our faith. How we clothe it depends upon our outlook. Is God a demeaning super dictator who demands strict rules to follow? Or do you visualize this Creator as one who sees delight in the newly emerging rosebud or the giggling child? Of seeing people discovering the joy of creating something new, be it an idea or a piece of cloth?

We make decisions about who we are by our attitudes and demeanor. There are moments of disgust in myself when I fail to remember the name of a friend's sister who needs prayer. I could justify why I didn't take the time to remember it, but that doesn't work too well with my psyche. I know the truth. Still, I know that the Creator whom I love, loves me even if I may forget some important information. My friend has forgiven me as well.

Bring in the Clowns—
A Metaphor for Ministry

Bishop K. H. Ting of the Chinese Christian Council has a basic premise for his theology. It rings in the title of his book, which includes his writings over a period of great turmoil in China. Bishop Ting's title is simply, "*Love Never Ends.*" His writings through this tumultuous time reveal a specific thread. He wasn't talking just about a theological doctrine. He lived as if God's love never ends, even during the Cultural Revolution.

His life was clothed in that love, which allowed him to persist in times of deepest darkness. When you have that kind of perspective, you give hope to others. Encouragement is offered to carry on even in devastating situations.

Dr. Ting loved to quote Teilhard de Chardin: "Someday, after we have mastered the wind, the waves, the tide, and gravity, we shall harness for God the energies of love: and then, for the second time in the history of the world, man will have discovered fire."

This reminded me of the response Wrinkles and Doolotz had with those students in Jiangsu Bible School. They clothed each other with red dots of love allowing laughter to spread across the room. That kind of joy still resonates in these old clowns to this very moment. God's love can be contagious if we let it be caught by others.

Barbara Swicegood is a pastor's wife who learned clowning. She chose as her clown name and persona, "Pearlie." An older relative in the South whose name was

Clothing the Clown—
Where Ministry Takes You

Pearl had raised her. Barbara's costume was straight out of the 1930s and 1940s.

Her hat was reminiscent of the late Minnie Pearl's. Barbara's "Pearlie" had old brown women's stockings out of the 1930s, and they never were really straight. She wore an apron and used simple but effective makeup. She was as cute as she could be, both in costume and in personality. She also was a nonverbal clown.

Her character gave her permission to enter into situations that may have been off-limits to her as Barbara. She was one of the participants in one of Portland's special Rose Festival events, the Junior Rose Parade. It was mostly made up of students of all ages in a weekday noontime parade. Clowns, however, were welcome. Barbara set out to gently work the people in the parade.

As well as I can remember the incident, Pearlie slowly approached a local policeman as he sat on his motorcycle before the parade started. When she felt he had allowed her into a little of his "space," Pearlie stepped closer. With a little cloth she began to first polish the motorcycle's front fender.

Then with a little more courage, she dusted off the handlebars. Then with real daring, because the policeman was enjoying the attention, she even polished his police badge. Finally she blew a kiss and stepped away.

"I could never have done that as Barbara," she later confessed. "But with Pearlie it was easy. His eyes told me it was OK to get closer."

Bring in the Clowns–
A Metaphor for Ministry

Her "clothing" and her awareness of who was on stage gave her the permission. Pearlie was the audience and the policeman was on the stage.

THOUGHTS FOR YOUR REFLECTION

1. As a clergy person, how important is how you look? Your choice of hairstyle, and, if a man, facial hair? What are you trying to project? How do you respond to people who snicker at your choice of clothes or hairstyles? On a rating of 1-10, with 10 being most important, where do you place your personal style choices? What does this say to you?

2. If you're into clowning, how important is it for you to keep your costume clean and limited in personal smells? Often, we can be "smelled" before seen, especially if we use a lot of makeup and heavily powder down our makeup. Have you checked your deodorant, especially if you are going to be working closely with patients or other clowns?

    Early in our clowning we learned that, as clowns, you don't smoke or eat while in costume. Can you imagine why that was important? What does it do to see a clown in a bar or smoking while sitting in a van while others in the parade pass by? What kind of mystique is lost?

Clothing the Clown—
Where Ministry Takes You

Jesus was accused of eating and drinking with sinners and even with a prostitute who bathed his feet in her tears. How do you grasp that kind of strange behavior? Have you ever been caught out of character as a follower of Jesus? What kind of "picture" did you inscribe on another's memory?

4. More importantly, what were some of the experiences you had where you were able to understand people with whom you normally don't associate?

I think of a man who was at a large church convention and took a break. It was a hot Midwestern summer day. Because he wanted to have a cool glass of beer, he went into a nearby tavern. After he sat down, he noticed it was a topless bar, and one of the women came over to talk to him.

When she learned he was a person of faith, she began a counseling session right there in the bar. He was able to hear her share her concerns for the family she was raising alone and her concern for where she was employed.

How would you feel if that was you or if one of your laypersons told the story straight? This man told about the experience in a conversation with other church members. Jesus was a friend of sinners and outcasts. How comfortable are you in the "clothing" of ministry that would take you into situations that are contrary to what other members in the congregation expect?

5. If a clown, how free do you feel with your make-up and costume? Do you experiment with some ideas that you wouldn't try being "straight"? In what ways is this a dilemma? Does clowning and its clothing give you permission to do things you would never do when you are straight? What are the dangers in this sense of permission? Where do you find guidance?

6. In ministry, how creative are you willing to be? In what ways are you able to involve others in that process? Have you tried ideas similar to "imagineering"? What were they and how do you process the results? And are results as important as the process? How do you measure the difference? How willing are you to accept some ideas and programs that are outside your experience? With whom do you share those concerns?

Chapter 5

Going in
Unexpected Places
as Clowns and Clergy

A REMINDER FROM CLOWNING

Wrinkles and Zyppurr were heading down the hallway toward the emergency waiting room. We usually just went to those waiting to receive emergency treatment. But this time the doors to the emergency room suddenly opened widely. A desk clerk we had known on 2G flung open his arms and said, "C'mon in!" It was an unexpected welcome into a place where often heavy, right-now needs had to be met.

We were surprised by this invitation and proceeded with caution. Both of us have had our days as patients in ER, but this was a new experience as clowns. One that came without any advanced preparation. But in we went as adventurous clowns once again.

107

Bring in the Clowns—
A Metaphor for Ministry

What we discovered was that these patients were just as real as those on the cardiac ward from which we had just come. Of course, we should have known this. But with the excitement over the years from the "ER" TV program, we found it quite different.

The nurses, aides, and other personnel were quietly going about their responsibilities. Our task was to ask which patients might be able to handle a couple of clowns. The desk clerk would let us know. Since Providence Portland Hospital did not have a pediatric ward, most of the patients were adults. Occasionally, children were there accompanying a family member. It was a scary time for both the children and parents. But somehow, with a funny-looking couple of clowns, tensions often melted at least for a few minutes.

We were as surprised by their responses to our efforts in ER as we often have been during our regular visits on the other floors of the hospital. They were people who were hurting and needing special care. Many of them in ER would be released later in the day or evening. A few were of the trauma class, so we didn't visit them. They usually went on to the necessary floors of the hospital after tests were completed.

From that experience of "c'mon in" we learned an important lesson. When serendipities of the Spirit present themselves, be open to respond. Sometimes the action is "no" or "later," but a response is essential.

Going in Unexpected Places
as Clowns and Clergy

Check a few of Jesus' responses to unexpected happenings as he walked through his ministry; a short man in a sycamore tree, a blind man yelling out to him for help while everyone around him was telling him to "shut up." It was as if disciples and those around Jesus were trying to suggest who was most important and who could be ignored. Jesus seldom ignored those seeking help. He was the master of handling the unexpected.

THE UNEXPECTED IN PASTORAL MINISTRY

August of 1979 was pivotal for my ministry. For nine years I had been juggling two ministries. I had moved from an urban church in Portland to a suburban church in Portland. The shift in the two locales was almost traumatic. Kenilworth had middle to lower income people who were very loving and willing to create ministry. Sunset Presbyterian was suburbia with middle and upper income people. Would they be as open and willing as I found in the urban and less-formally-educated church.

At one time I had felt that the suburbs were the "enemy" for work in the city. So it was very strange to be called there. The pastor-seeking committee had attended Kenilworth on a Sunday when we were quite creative.

Balloons were all over the place, and the congregation was very involved. The service had been planned by the worship committee. I'm not sure what the occasion was, but I rather suspect it had something to do with joy in the Spirit. It could have been an outcome from some prose written by Ann Weems asserting, "Balloons belong in church."

This was hardly the time one would expect to find a pastor-seeking committee. To be honest, the service was joyfully funky! The congregation thought the committee people were possibly new members, so they welcomed them with open arms. The committee had discretely mingled with the congregation.

Had I known there was a pastor-seeking committee present or was planning to come, I suspect I would have chosen another kind of service. But then again, why should I have thought that way? You are what you create, so why not have balloons in church? The worship committee had done its job and we rejoiced.

This is but another step in being open to the unexpected. Planning and executing those plans within the church are the basics of good stewardship. Time, talents, and gifts of the Spirit direct ministries and lead to some interesting experiences to savor.

A few weeks later, a call was presented to me from Sunset Presbyterian Church. That was in 1970, but what lay ahead were some experiences in ministry that helped with the pivotal year of 1979.

Going in Unexpected Places as Clowns and Clergy

Discovering "golden"
OPPORTUNITIES IN LEADERSHIP

One of the basic factors in my ministry was to share leadership. There were elders who few would have considered as being capable of leadership, but they delivered it. What they really wanted was the opportunity. The other elders and I gave them support when they needed it.

Ike was one of those elders in the small urban church. He was usually found handing out stamps and checking packages at the Post Office. With a little training and encouragement, he became a stalwart leader in stewardship in the church. He worked with his committee and helped launch the stewardship program for remodeling the sanctuary.

Another unlikely man became the elder for Mission who pushed us to be aware of the world outside of Kenilworth. He was a bit brusque in his manners, but given the job, he worked very hard at it. Ben rallied the congregation to be supportive of mission beyond its borders.

Kenilworth was a place where members and friends were given the opportunity to be involved. The remodeling of the sanctuary, its third movement within the framework of the building, was such a case.

A baker, Dick discovered he liked to search out the furniture for the new sanctuary. Since he worked odd hours, usually at night, he was available to research both the needs and the possibilities. He ended up going to a Trappist monastery in Oregon where the good brothers not only prayed a lot, but also made wonderful furniture.

Since the good brothers also raised most of their own grains, they made wonderful bakery goods. Dick did some baking with them as well. But it was the sleek and beautiful dark mahogany wood furniture that was his fascination.

At the dedication of the remodeled sanctuary, even the priest from the Trappist Monastery came. This was barely after the Vatican II experience and interfaith relations were just beginning to open up. His presence was most unusual, but well received. He delighted in seeing how the talented Trappists' products added to the worship dimensions of the sanctuary.

Other people in the congregation who were skilled with their hands also helped put much sweat labor into the remodeling. One family, whose oldest son was in an almost constant coma, made the unique light fixtures.

The family would take their son and put him on protected foam mattress in the canopied bed of their truck and then go rock hunting. They traveled all over the northwest and discovered some marvelous agates and minerals. Many rocks had significant scriptural background.

Going in Unexpected Places
as Clowns and Clergy

In turn, the family sliced and polished them. Then using three-pound round oatmeal boxes for molds, they began to make the individual lights. Each of them contained slices of rocks that became translucent when the lights were switched on.

Lights were hung in the narthex and a marvelous chandelier in the sanctuary. They became a memorial to their teenage son who had died by the time the sanctuary was completed.

These were skilled laborers who were part of the church and, along with many others, shared their gifts. Duane was one of the professional men in the church. By profession he was an electrical engineer. By commitment he was the clerk of Session, a post he held or helped with for more than forty years.

Bring in the Clowns—
A Metaphor for Ministry

He was willing to serve, even though many weeks he would be on location at large electrical sites. But even as important, he served in FISH, a local program to assist the poorest of the community with food and other provisions.

As a Mississippi-born transplant, Duane was most open in accepting many people who became a part of the church. There were some whose skin tones were far different from his own. His was a stellar voice of reason and often questioned the clergy about the direction of faith's actions and inclusions. Duane set the table for gracious acceptance.

For me, he, along with others in that congregation, provided a unique opportunity. We were an integrated congregation at a time when even in a northern city like Portland, Oregon, this was a bit unusual. What it did for our family was to give them the chance to have close school friends and no concern for their ethnic origin. As a family we moved into that marvelous and unexpected place of being accepted by others whose origins were far different from our own.

Thus it was difficult to seriously consider the move to the suburbs. Our daughter was going to be a senior in Cleveland High School that following fall. Hers would be a difficult transition from urban to suburban schools. There was to be some resistance because her friends were in southeast Portland and we were moving to northwest Portland about fifteen miles away.

Going in Unexpected Places as Clowns and Clergy

One of the questions I asked of Sunset Church was if they were willing to let me continue to produce the Open Door radio program. Since it was geared to youth, the congregation's response was to continue doing it. This is what eventually led to a pivotal decision nine years later.

DIFFICULT CHOICES IN MINISTRY

One of the most challenging statements the pastor-seeking committee had made caused me to ponder. One of them said words to the effect that they had been struggling. They'd had a good eighteen months with an older interim pastor who had brought the congregation back together. Now they challenged me by saying, "You may be our last pastor."

I'm not sure if they meant I'd be there until I retired, or more accurately that they weren't sure they would survive as a congregation. Was it an invitation to disaster and ultimately the burying of a congregation? I've been up to a number of challenges, but this was one that caused serious consternation. Yet the Spirit seemed to say, "Go for it Bud. You're not alone!" That proved to be the case not just for me, but for the congregation.

Over the nine years, the Sunset congregation was quite open to the kinds of innovations committees brought together. On a beautiful sunny Friday and Saturday afternoon, local artists came and displayed their wares. Some of them were from the church, but others were part of that struggling artist scene. They were largely young men and women wanting to share their creative gifts, many wondering if this would be a way to become successful.

One of those sharing his talents and goods was a neighbor of ours. He was a skillful potter, but his subjects were usually very large. He created eight-foot chess men or large bathtubs! At Sunset he just brought things like bowls and tea sets. But it was a time of exposure. While he never became a part of the church, our contacts of friendship lasted during the years we lived close to him. A large Aladdin-like teapot is a reminder of Joel Cottet's talents.

Innovation in worship was a constant. One of the long-time members of Sunset once said, "Bud, we never know exactly what to expect on Sunday morning, but we're excited to come." We had drama in the sanctuary. Our choir put together a rock rendition of the creation story. We taped it ahead of time and then matched slides to go with the music. That way the choir along with the congregation could enjoy the experience in worship.

One Christmas Eve, Lenore and our oldest son Chris pantomimed the lovely Peter, Paul, and Mary song, *"The Christmas Dinner."* A friend from another church, Carolyn Birt, played her guitar and sang to their actions.

At this time we had a growing youth group, and the neighborhood youngsters around the church needed a place to play. The church grounds were quite large. The

Going in Unexpected Places
as Clowns and Clergy

Session and the trustees decided that what might be needed was a place to play basketball. With the trustees planning the details, a large concrete slab was laid down a little larger than the size of a basketball court. That way other sports could be used on it. Lovingly we called it, "The Slab."

Many an afternoon in the spring through summer months found several young people playing hoops. It was an outreach into the community.

The church grounds also went into a wooded section, so the congregation again planned a way to creatively use it during the summer. Since I had received summer day-camp training, we designed a day camp experience for about thirty fourth to sixth grade students. The idea was that many of these youth could not afford to go to an overnight camping experience. By having it held on the church grounds, a wholesome experience was available to church youth and their friends. They could sleep in their own beds at night.

We managed to have three "home" groups led by a couple of adults and ten young people. They spent the day in Bible study, nature walks, games, and even cookouts, because the church had a great patio that was safe for fires. There were also the usual summer camp crafts. But the youth went home for supper and to sleep.

Day camp was just another of the alternatives that summertime could offer to the children and youth of the church. In my ministry at First Presbyterian Church

Bring in the Clowns—
A Metaphor for Ministry

in Stockton, California, I had become acquainted with mission trips. That was something quite innovative in the early 1960s. I had been a part of six or eight of them during my time in Stockton, going to places in Utah, Idaho, and California.

It was something we had also done at Kenilworth. We trained our youth so they could also teach summer Bible school on the mission trip. Usually it also meant doing some physical work with the church plant where we stayed.

The idea was a bit new to the Sunset congregation, but there was a spirit of adventure among the young people and their leaders. With much planning, youth and adult leadership led a number of mission trips.

One summer it meant traveling by cars to a port in Canada where we boarded an inland ferry to Sitka, Alaska. There the youth painted houses and helped with the growing aquaculture project of Sheldon Jackson College. The youth and advisors had so much fun the adults who heard the story said, "How can we do this?"

Again, creative minds were at work within the congregation. Families and youth signed up for a mission trip of both adults and youth to Alaska. The journey was to be on board the Presbyterian Church's own ship, the Anna Jackman. That ship traveled the inland passages to various outposts of the church in Alaska. There they helped small communities where churches were struggling to minister.

Going in Unexpected Places
as Clowns and Clergy

The chaplain on board, Rev. Ward Murray, doubled as clergy, crew, cook, and various other tasks that would suddenly come his way. Lenore and I had known Ward when he pastored a church near Stockton, California. So for us it was an opportunity to work together again in ministry.

By now, Lenore and I had been into a little bit of clowning, so one of the events that the mission trip crew planned was the celebration of Wally and Shirley Masters twenty-fifth wedding anniversary. It was to be different as you might expect.

When we docked at a logging camp for an overnight stay, we invited the people in the camp to come aboard for our clown wedding. Members of the Sunset Church took the parts of pastor, best man, maid of honor, flower girl, ushers, soloist, plus the bride and groom.

The difference was that the whole service was done in pantomime. All the people from Sunset were "in face." Lenore and I helped them, but most put on their own clown faces. I'm not sure how the people from the logging camp enjoyed it, but there was no doubt in the minds of those who planned it. An account of the story made the front page with a large photo in the area newspaper near Sunset Church.

That was another example of being open to the unexpected in ministry, no matter where we are. Yes, it is a bit risky, and sometimes the results are not what we expect. They can fall very flat. But at the same time, there

Bring in the Clowns—
A Metaphor for Ministry

Wedding Pantomime in Alaska Trip anniversary

are those from the Anna Jackman trip, who years later fondly remembered the experience as a highlight.

PLANNED EXCEPTIONS

At both Kenilworth and Sunset churches, the Sessions allowed me to pursue pastoral exchanges. At Kenilworth, the St. Andrews Presbyterian Church in Geelong, Victoria, Australia sent their pastor, Rev Bill Littler and his wife for a six month stay. That meant my family of five, plus a cousin, traveled to Geelong. The experience was one that eventually led our youngest son Todd on his many overseas teaching assignments. Later, he also offered us unexpected opportunities for sharing clowning.

Sunset Church encouraged the summer exchange with Pastor Frank Nunn of Sheffield, Yorkshire,

Going in Unexpected Places
as Clowns and Clergy

England. He brought his family with him, while our high-school and college-age children stayed in Portland. This trip allowed me to do some extended work in media at St. Gabriel's media center in Hatch End, just outside of London.

What these kinds of pastoral exchanges allowed for the congregation and us were opportunities to gain greater perspective on the world. All too often we become "navel watchers," zeroed in on our church navels instead of visioning the world. This was meant to be a two-way street for both congregations. The world became a tiny bit smaller with these visitations, both for the people in the churches and for the pastors and their families.

Opportunities are out there if one has the courage to think them possible. When we as a family planned to head to Australia, we had to make sacrifices. Since the planning took over a year to consummate, the Christmas before leaving was quite simple in our home.

Our two young sons, Chris and Todd, who were still in elementary school, had been earning money with a weekly community newspaper they distributed. They even went out when the streets were icy and the local Portland daily paper wasn't delivered! Their patrons were very generous in their payments.

Margaret set about for her own moneymaking. As a fourteen year old she tried selling cosmetics door to door. Baby sitting was a much more reliable source of income.

Bring in the Clowns—
A Metaphor for Ministry

She, along with the rest of the family, was saving every possible cent she could for the trip to Australia.

The Christmas prior to our leaving, we had one of the best celebrations possible. Our Christmas presents were all tucked into savings. We enjoyed the time knowing that a trip of a lifetime to Australia was a six-month present for all to enjoy. A cousin, David Beck, joined us for the experience.

That trip happened in 1969. It was a planned experience, but with many unexpected opportunities that arose as serendipities of the Spirit. Not only had the interracial church experience at Kenilworth affected us all, but now the larger world view came into our perspectives. That awareness continues in all of our family's lives.

So the call in ministry is to do some planned "unexpecteds" to test your fortitude. More importantly, they can expand your faith's understanding. When Jesus calls us to "come, follow me," that sometimes can mean clear directions. But more often, it brings the unexpected that challenges our book learning of faith.

HARD CHOICES OFTEN LEAD
TO UNEXPECTED DESTINATIONS

During the years at Sunset Presbyterian, the Open Door radio program began to consume more of my time. Not only was the program heard on several related Portland stations, but with the station's help, the program was being heard in other cities. That led to more time

Going in Unexpected Places
as Clowns and Clergy

being spent on planning the well-scripted program to make it meet the standards of the industry.

This also meant finding the time to write and then produce the thirty-minute prose and music program. As most clergy know, our normal work week is around fifty or more hours. By the very nature of our calling, we are open to being on call, much like physicians. Family crises occur and you are called out of bed in the wee hours of the morning. It comes with the calling.

I added to that number of hours in pastoral ministry the work of the radio program. By industry standards, the old saying was, "For every minute on air you need an hour of planning." That meant that somehow I had to discover at least an additional thirty hours of working time to do both jobs.

The work at Sunset paid the bills. The work at 62KGW was volunteer, although later I was paid all of $25/week to produce the program. But the studios and the music libraries were open to me. I even had a key to the front door of the building that housed two radio stations and a top TV station! They gave me a picture ID card as well.

But where did the thirty hours come from? Usually they started about 9:00 P.M. each night and went for a

Going in Unexpected Places
as Clowns and Clergy

number of hours. Most church meetings need to be over by 9:00 o'clock, so it was pretty safe for me to be home. I'd listen to my growing rock 'n roll music library, mostly promotional singles, albums, and later CDs.

Themes would be suggested by the writings from our listeners. They were wide ranging in scope, but all reflecting concerns of the listeners. In essence, like in clowning, I was the audience, the listeners were on stage.

Thus, it meant working very long hours, but I had plenty of Type A motivation. Besides, I was enjoying this means of outreach in mainstream media.

Perhaps the most telling and somewhat whimsical experience at working these crazy long hours happened with our son Todd. He was about fifteen or sixteen. My office was in a basement room adjacent to his bedroom. The family room was next to my office. I had racks of albums lining the family room walls.

The "Hi-Fi" as we called it then, was in the family room. So I would listen to various cuts of the albums to check lyrics and time them. Late one night, about half past midnight, I was playing an album, most likely a little too loudly.

Todd staggered out of his bedroom. His eyes squinted by the sudden change from bedroom darkness to the bright florescent lighting of the family room. Looking at me he said the most revealing words a father could ever hear,

"Dad, would you turn down the Hi-Fi? I can't sleep!"

Bring in the Clowns—
A Metaphor for Ministry

Talk about a turn-around experience. That was it.

I had to turn that whole experience in another direction, but I didn't know how. I loved both the pastoral ministry and the extension of that ministry through radio. Quite quickly I learned that the so-called "glamour" of media had to be spelled W-O-R-K and lots of it.

Open Door had now grown to airing on fifty or sixty rock stations across the United States. Some interest was shown by the Armed Forces Radio network of stations as well. More and more of my "spare" time was being put into the workings of Open Door. All the time I kept to my fifty-plus hours of work in Sunset Church.

It was apparent to others, and somewhat denied by me, that I was working toward a real crisis. That is when the pivotal moments became apparent in August of 1979.

Lenore's family members from Iowa and California came for a visit. Since they were talking mostly about what had happened within the family in years past, I felt I could slip away to do some Open Door work. It was a Saturday afternoon and I was a bit troubled.

I went into my little office in the basement. It now became my home recording studio. The conversation going on in the living room upstairs was not where I was. I was having trouble concentrating on what was best for my ministry and me. I felt caught between two "goods"—the pastoral ministry and the radio ministry.

Going in Unexpected Places
as Clowns and Clergy

In my worst moments I almost wished that I'd have a heart attack so someone else would have to make the decision for me. A decision had to be made sometime soon.

The fact that I was this desperate in my emotional state, I certainly wasn't in a good position to make a reasonable decision. Years later I did have a heart attack, so my muddled thinking just didn't know what I was asking in terms of relief.

Here I was, with a wonderful family, in a church that needed even more of my attention than I could give it. The church was the place for my income. To top it off, all three of our children were now in private colleges. The calling was to stay at Sunset because of the financial support it provided. Open Door was struggling to find money to pay for expense of tapes, mailing, and all that went into that process.

The only way out seemed to be if I had a serious illness. Then others who were much more trustworthy than I was could help us out.

In my consternation and tears of frustration I heard a voice say,

"Trust me."

That couldn't have been from me because I certainly wasn't trustworthy to make any decisions. But the words still cause chills within me as I recall them that August afternoon in 1979. *"Trust me."*

Bring in the Clowns—
A Metaphor for Ministry

Within the next month, with the help of the Presbytery led by a friend Rev. Randy Riggs, the Session met to hammer out whatever decision that was to be made.

Elder Dick, a 6' 7" school superintendent and member of the Session said words that hang on in memory to this day, just as clearly as I heard them that early fall evening.

"Bud, what you're doing is ludicrous. You aren't fair to Sunset Church, to Open Door, or to your family. Somehow you've got to make up your mind for the sake of all of us."

I don't remember all the spin that went on with the rest of the meeting with the Session, but I offered my resignation effective the end of the year. I wondered if what I had heard, "*Trust me*," was genuine. But that was the risk I was about to take.

Lenore had said before that meeting, "Bud, do as you feel called to do, but know that I love you no matter what you decide. I'll go back into the work force to help us out."

She did and got a part-time job! But later it developed into an incredible ministry that used her gifts and talents in dimensions we never imagined.

The last service of worship I conducted as a pastor of a local church occurred on the last Sunday of December 1979. Then it was the step into the financial unknown— the exciting new unexpected venture into mass media full time. It was a pivotal time for my family and ministry.

Going in Unexpected Places
as Clowns and Clergy

We were heading into unknown and sometimes scary territory of ministry. But somehow, both Lenore and I knew it was a step that had to be taken.

"*Trust me*" was what I heard. I had to respond. So did the Spirit.

QUESTIONS TO CONSIDER

1. Consider checking the unexpected incidents that confronted Jesus in his ministry. How did he handle a bungled healing by the disciples while he was away in prayer? What was his attitude? Find places where he was interrupted in going about his ministry, like a woman at Jacob's well. Was she the greatest subject to become the first evangelist to her village where she had been shunned?

Where have you been stunned by people whom you certainly didn't expect to be receptive to the gospel? What if they looked different, spoke with a different accent? Where does the gospel force you to travel that you are reluctant to go?

2. Perhaps one of the hardest places for both clowns and clergy to go is into the area of physical fitness. Both callings are demanding of physical energies.

Bring in the Clowns—
A Metaphor for Ministry

How are you caring for your body? As one who has gone through heart bypass surgery, I finally discovered that regular physical exercise is essential. Are you into some kind of regular routine that gets you out of a comfortable chair? My pastor, Jim Moiso, has had quadruple heart bypass surgery. Now early every morning he is on the sidewalks with long walks. He monitors his physical needs and watches his diet regularly.

How are you handling your diet? So many of us pastors claim our weight gains are due to all the pot-luck meals we attend, but is it really that we don't want to challenge our eating habits? For your own health and that of the congregation, look for ways to be active with your body. Typing on the keyboard of the computer doesn't do it. You might even want to go regularly to a gym. Early in the day will help you with your mental and spiritual health. How many times have you said, "I ought to do this"? As a well-known sports apparel commercial notes, "Just do it."

The gym may be one of the most unexpected places you'll discover. How will you share the gospel there as a new option? Friend Dennis Benson has become a gym "rat" where he has become a friend of other gym "rats." But he also has friends he meets almost daily in a local café. They also have welcomed him. Can you think of places where you can meet people outside of your church family, maybe for coffee? Or how often do you plan a time for lunch or coffee break with church members?

Going in Unexpected Places
as Clowns and Clergy

If you are doing clowning, you know how very taxing it can be on all your faculties. An hour of "being on" greatly enervates you. How do you recuperate and go on, especially if you have a gig that requires more time?

In our hospital clown ministry, we're "on" for up to four hours. That's one of the reasons we both "hit the floor" right after getting out of bed in the mornings. We do stretching exercises physical therapists have suggested. This happens even before we make it to the breakfast table.

How can you develop a regimen that fits your lifestyle? How willing are you to tap into all of your bodily needs this way? Where will you look for opportunities to nurture God's good gift of a complete body? Will you discover how the mind and spirit will likewise be uplifted because your body is functioning better?

Life is filled with all kinds of daily and often hourly interruptions. Jesus was master of dealing with them, yet also caring for himself. This might be an unexpected place for you to move, be it as a clown or clergy or one of God's other wondrous people.

Chapter 6
Space—It's More Than Air

Avner the Eccentric is a marvelous human being and entertainer. But he is also an excellent instructor. In the early 1980s Lenore and I went to a National Clown, Mime, Puppet, and Dance Ministry Workshop in Berkeley, California. It was held on the campus of the University of California. Avner was one of the teachers.

This gathering of several hundred men and women from all over the West brought together leaders with special gifts. For us, Avner's was the understanding of space.

A recent incident brought to mind the importance of that word. We were visiting our daughter, Margaret, in Astoria, Oregon. On that weekend there was a parade marking a special time in the city's year. Included were

Bring in the Clowns— A Metaphor for Ministry

all kinds of floats, marching bands, and an assortment of other characters.

One large float was shaped like a pirate ship. Time and again as it traveled down the streets they would set off an extremely loud cannon, not with explosives, but just powder and awesome sound.

Accompanying the ship were pirate clowns. They swooped down upon the people lining the route, swishing shining plastic swords close up to people, especially children, scaring them. They went right up to children's faces and yelled to scare them, then left laughing.

Probably they thought they were doing their job as pirates, but they certainly did not understand personal space. They also provided children with the idea that clowns are monsters of whom to be afraid.

Avner taught us differently. He instructed us to look into the eyes of those who have gained your attention. Watch their faces as you come closer. How do they respond? Can you sense a receptivity or "don't come any closer" feeling?

He reminded us, as clowns, that about an arm's length is as close as most people want you to come. Coming in closer without their permission can cause problems, one of which might be a shove to keep you away. Their space is considered sacred to them, and we need to be aware not to violate it.

This is true in most of our relationships when we are in a group that is standing around. Our body language speaks loudly if people are listening. No words need to be said. Sometimes the other person will turn the other way from you, not a major slight, but just the statement that "You're invading my personal space."

Bring in the Clowns—
A Metaphor for Ministry

When clowning in the hospital, this is most important. Patients often feel they have no control. Doctors and nurses are the ones who provide the instructions to what the patient needs.

An intruder, like a clown, must ask permission before entering a patient's room. This is one of the only times during their stay in the hospital that patients have control. This empowers them.

As clowns we gently tap on their door, whether open or closed. If invited in, we just take a few steps in so the patient can decide whether or not she or he wants a couple of clowns. We will ask, "Would you like a couple of clowns to come in for a few minutes?"

Most often, the patients are curious enough to wonder what a couple of old clowns like us are doing there, so we are welcomed in. While clowning in the hospital, we break from our silence on many occasions so we can both listen to the patient and respond.

Often, we find that men are the most hesitant to have clowns in their room. I think this speaks a great deal to us men folk about our inability to set aside our macho control mechanisms. "How dare you even think of bringing smiles to this dadgumed hospital room..." (They might use different words.)

But the "man" issue can be contested, because some of the warmest welcomes and experiences we've had have come from men. Here is one that touches us deeply.

Space—It's More Than Air

Wrinkles and Zyppurr were at the last room on 2G, I call it the Cardiac Ward because many of the patients are cardiac patients. It is really the "Telemetry" floor. Patients' hearts are being monitored by the electronic devices they wear.

But when we looked into this last room, there sat a man on the edge of his bed with his feet dangling. His hands were on a folder on his bedside table. He was dressed in the usual hospital gowns.

I looked at him and figured, here's another man who will not want to have a couple of clowns come in. After all, we had had several men in other rooms say no to our entering that day.

He was a man with short, cropped white hair and large tattoos on his bulging biceps. An inch-long white beard was neatly trimmed. For all appearances I figured he was a "tough guy" who certainly wouldn't be interested in a couple of bright-eyed and colorful clowns. Someone has said that fear hinders creativity. Or, as I like to think, the uncertainty of a situation often energizes the spirit and you can move on.

Zyppurr asked, "Would you like us to come in?" I expected a gruff "No!"

Instead, he simply nodded for us to enter. As we noted things in his room, we responded to a breathing device that was on his bedside table. Our little shtick in the room was to use a similar device I had been given when I was a patient. It is used to help patients expand their lungs after surgery and to clear them of any remnants of the anesthetics.

As Zyppurr, I suggested that I had the proper technique for using the device and wanted him to observe. As Zyppurr sucked on the device a little measure would rise to indicate how strongly I sucked in air. The idea is to get it to the top, which I eventually did. Then, turning aside from the patient, I punched my belly and blew on the pinwheel.

We've done that little routine for over nine years and we don't understand why people giggle after I've done it. But they do. And he did. We then offered him a homemade pinwheel that Wrinkles had made.

She uses a #2 wooden pencil, some brightly colored paper, a tiny bead as a bearing, and a one-inch sewing pin with a colorful head. Piecing it altogether, she attaches the pin, bead and "blades" of the pinwheel to the rubber eraser on the end of the pencil.

She asked this man which one of about a half dozen different colored pinwheels would he like. After choosing the pinwheel, Zyppurr offered to attach that pinwheel to his breathing device. It was then that we learned something new.

He responded, "You don't need to do it. You see, you gave me one of these the last time I was here. And I still have it."

We hadn't realized we had seen him before because it could have been months or years before. I felt a little strange about this experience. We hadn't remembered that previous visit. So I reached into my basket and pulled out a red sponge nose. I wanted to give him something new from us.

As I offered this new gift to him I said, "I'll show you how to put it on."

He responded, "You don't have to. You see, I'm also a clown!"

But that wasn't the last of the experience. He went on to say how much he had appreciated our first visit and then continued, "But you won't see me here again. You see, I'm dying."

Wrinkles and Zyppurr both took a quick deep breath as he went on to say, "I'm not worried about dying. Take a look at this notebook I have on my table. Here are pictures of my wife who died just a couple of years ago. These are our marriage and family pictures."

Then he turned a couple of pages more.

"This is my memorial service. I've planned it all with my pastor and the church. I'm not afraid. I'm ready."

When Wrinkles offered him one of her "Free Hug" certificates, he immediately wanted to share a hug with her.

When we left the room, we were breathing new air. The breath of the living God was gently caressing our spirits. We walked with a lighter and deeply appreciative step down the hall. A new space was made in our memory banks.

Bring in the Clowns—
A Metaphor for Ministry

This wonderful human being had lifted us, we who had entered the room to provide some gentle cheer! But it also was a wonderful reminder for us of two clown and ministry basics:

1. We allowed him to be in charge. He was the one on stage and we were the audience.
2. He understood the meaning of space. He defined it by allowing us in. He also described that distance when he gave Wrinkles a hug.

In the previous chapter, I wrote about my asking Sarah to teach me how to hug. It was a question about space for me. Sarah easily answered that request with an action that defined what she saw as space.

PLAY SPACES

Do you have a "Holy Play Sunday" in your church? Maybe you call it by another name, like "Bright Sunday." It's an old tradition that Cal Samra of *The Fellowship of Joyful Christians* literally resurrected for the church.

Bright Sunday is the Sunday following Easter. According to Cal, it began centuries ago in medieval times. The reason for the celebration was that following the awe-filled experience of "Good" Friday when the devil felt he had won the battle with God, Easter proved him wrong.

Space—It's More Than Air

God had played a joke on the devil. Jesus was resurrected. Darkness was changed to brightness, so it became a time of celebration.

Many churches celebrated on Monday after Easter with people sharing jokes, telling stories, and sometimes playing funny pranks on each other. Often the priests were the focal point of the humor.

Somehow the tradition got lost, perhaps with the more harsh theology of the reformers who wanted to counterattack the frivolities of the dominant Roman Catholic traditions. Even the Catholics settled in for more ritual forms and "Bright" Monday or Sunday was lost.

But here came Cal Samara to the rescue. In his *The Joyful Noiseletter* publication, he promoted returning to this celebration. This is a marvelous resource for pastors and clowns, if they're not one and the same. It includes many wonderful clean jokes, cartoons, and endearing articles shared by readers. Contact him at JoyfulNZ@ aol.com for more information about the newsletter.

Many churches now have these kinds of post-Easter celebrations. At Westminster Presbyterian Church in Portland, Oregon, where we attend, this kind of celebration has been going on for a number of years.

One year, just as the pastor was stepping into the chancel area for the announcements, one of the deacons rolled a basketball down the center aisle. When it gently bounced off the front step, Pastor Moiso said, "That's the first time I've seen a holy roller in a Presbyterian church." Holy Humor Sunday had begun.

People were encouraged to wear their favorite outrageous clothing. Men wore the ties they normally never wanted to be seen wearing. Women wore strange-colored wigs. Children came with wonder at what was happening in such a place. Clowns were greeting and escorting parishioners to their pews. Balloons were posted everywhere. Paper airplanes came floating down from the balcony at one place in the service. All kinds of creative and imaginative ways were used to lessen the space between worshipers, either in actual physical dimensions or socially. The choir came down the center aisle with numbers attached to the back of their choir robes like basketball players. The inference was that you can't tell who the singer was without a program with a number in it.

That choir added some extra humor after the pastor of the morning completed his sermon. Members stood up with large cardboard signs with numbers on them, much like the judging ice skaters receive. There was no doubt about what kind of reaction the congregation gave to this sight.

It also brought a sense of the depth of humor God offered through his Son. Remember when the disciples wanted to keep the little children from scrambling through the legs of the adults to get to Jesus? The disciples tried to stop them. They were trying to protect

Jesus' space, i.e. for adults only. But Jesus would have none of that.

"Let the children come to me, for of such is the kingdom of God." (Luke 18:15-17) The fact that the children wanted to be close to Jesus tells us how open his invitation was to them. He may not have said a word to them, but children have that "sixth sense." They knew that if they could get through the maze of adult legs, arms, and "no's," they would be welcomed into Jesus' space and possibly onto his lap.

I'd like to have seen the faces of the disciples when Jesus encouraged the children to come to him. Jesus was making his space vulnerable to them. I wonder what tales those children later told to their children! Would they have been that open to not only their own children, but others?

Bring in the Clowns—
A Metaphor for Ministry

Jesus burst the bubble of God being distant. Jesus brought God up close. Our theology speaks of the Trinity being three in one. We may want to keep God at a distance, but Yahweh can't be contained "up" or "out there." Jesus, once and for all, closed that gap.

We are often confused about how the Trinity could describe God. How could three in one be possible? Too often we consider it a matter of addition. That is, one plus one plus one, i.e. Father, Son, Holy Spirit. Someone suggested that what we really need is to see the Trinity, not as addition, but multiplication. One times One times One still equals One! One God in three persons, blessed Trinity.

The gift of the third person in the Trinity continues to tell us there is no space between God and us. We are the ones who have to adjust. I don't see this triune God as the big eye in the sky. This God is as close as our breath. How surprising that God has always closed the space between who God is and us. We are the ones "on stage" who chose to allow that space to become greater or less. God does not force a closure of distance.

Check out the web site http://www.*JOYFUL-NOISELETTER.COM* for more information on how to celebrate Holy Humor or Holy Play Sunday. You'll find a great many ideas to entice your own creative juices to flow. This is just another reminder of finding space for holy, wholesome play within the community of faith.

Space—It's More Than Air

HOW CLOSE IS CLOSE?

Check the scene in John 13. It is a time of preparations for the Last Supper. Jesus became the servant to his followers. No one else had washed the disciples' feet. Jesus became the host for the meal. As host he was the one who took the towel and the bowl of water. He knelt in front of each disciple, even Judas Iscariot. There Jesus washed the gritty, road-dusty feet. What can be more humbling than washing another person's feet? But also, how very refreshing it is for whom the feet are washed.

Have you been on a retreat where you might have read this passage and then had participants wash one another's feet? I remember a deacons' retreat to the Oregon beach. These were mostly women. We had read the Scriptures and all of us were either sitting on chairs or on the floor.

A basin of warm water was made available. As we washed each other's feet, there was a warm glow in the room. Clean feet, cleared of those incredibly tiny grains of gritty sand, felt wonderful. Some deacons even brought a little lotion with which to massage the feet following the washing and drying.

When it was my turn to wash one woman's feet, I noticed she had on panty hose! What was I to do as a male pastor? All the deacons knew that foot washing was going to happen before we shared the Lord's Supper.

Bring in the Clowns—
A Metaphor for Ministry

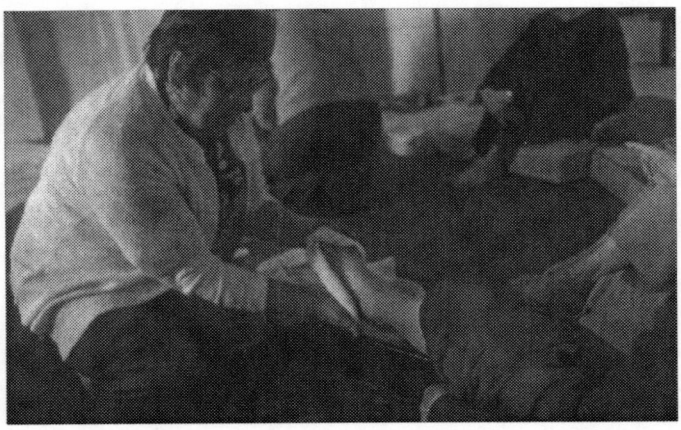

But here she was with unremovable panty hose, at least in the presence of all the deacons.

She said, "Just go ahead and wash my feet. Don't worry about the panty hose, they'll dry quickly."

We all had a chuckle about that one. This pixie-like older woman delighted in seeing how I would handle this dilemma. So did the rest of the deacons. So did I, because I strongly remember the experience some thirty years later...and smile.

The significance of foot washing was giving permission to another person to move into a very close space for accepted touching. We could have washed each other's hands. No doubt you have been in Maundy Thursday services where that happened.

But the lowly, gritty, sand-filled feet—that's a whole other dimension of intimacy. Jesus' simple action honored each disciple. It was the intimacy of service and servitude. (Read again Philippians 2:1-11.)

Space—It's More Than Air

Friend Dennis Benson told of an experience of foot washing that moved him greatly.

"I thought of my dad's last days. I went to see him, and a woman was on her knees washing his feet. I said, 'There is someone else who washed feet.' She just smiled. When my dad died, this volunteer wrote me a note saying, 'It was an honor to wash your father's feet.'"

Most of us have difficulty comprehending that kind of space. Especially as we consider the consequences Jesus confronted later that same night. Indeed, his identity with us gives a rise to awesome hope. It also leads us to another dimension of space.

SPACE AS A MEDIUM OF FAITH

The wife of our senior pastor, Jim Moiso, suffered a reoccurrence of her cancer. It had been more than five years since she had surgery for breast cancer. It returned in another more-pervasive form. But typical of the grit of these two devoted people, they wanted to challenge this scourge.

Incredibly difficult and trying procedures were attempted with slim lasting responses. The congregation was very aware of their concerns, but they were not going to give up without exploring as many avenues of medication as possible.

Jim and his wife Linda heard about a Taizé Healing and Wholeness service. It was held the second Sunday evening of the month at Holy Trinity Episcopal Cathedral in Portland. They began attending regularly.

Shortly afterward, a young man began attending worship at Westminster. One day he came to talk with Jim. He said words to the effect, "I'm a healer. I've come to offer to pray with you and Linda."

This was most unusual for a mainline church. Our vision of a healer was one of the TV evangelists, very staged. Whether we believed their outcomes or not, it just was not what we wanted.

Yet, Pastor Moiso welcomed Deryl Godshall into his study. Over a period of time Deryl, Jim, and Linda would meet regularly for prayer and the laying on of hands. Eventually this was enlarged to a number of Linda's closest friends who took part in the sessions offering their prayers and touches for healing.

Jim and Linda continued attending the healing and wholeness services at Holy Trinity Episcopal Cathedral. Jim wondered if the church he was serving would welcome this very different form of worship. He learned from his research that the reformed tradition had little to say about gifts of healing. Some of the early reformers were opposed to such claims. Yet, there was biblical evidence for prayers for healing, the anointing with oil, and laying on of hands. (See James 5:14 as a beginning place.)

Using the regular Presbyterian process of corporate decisions, committees and then Session consideration, a plan was ready for action. The careful planning, discussion, and willingness to trust the movement of the Holy Spirit led to the decision to act. The service was given a formal OK.

The Taizé Healing and Wholeness service was carefully designed. It uses the music from the Taizé Community with added prayers and Scripture reading. Five minutes of silence follow the Scripture lesson. For many of us, this was an unknown space. A sanctuary with people in it, sitting in silence. No soft music played. Just the incredible sacrament of silent space. A pause of quiet reflection and restoration.

Then there is a time for four prayers by whomever is leading, a pastor or one of the prayer team. Each prayer is followed by singing one verse of Taize-like music. It also includes a long printed list of people, places, and concerns. These are submitted in the weeks before the service. The names are read in unison and lifted to God as a common prayer by all at the service.

The service continues with Taizé music being sung or hummed, led by a small group of singers from the choir. The whole fifty-voice choir would be far too many. Only six-to-eight persons compose the Taize choir. They bring special vocal talents as well as several instruments. The music is almost like a sacred chant, repeating the two or three lines of the song up to eight times.

While the singing continues, the laying on of hands and anointing takes place. People come forward to one of three prayer kneelers. Two small stools are also next to two kneelers for those who cannot kneel. Thus, people can stand, sit, or kneel.

Two prayer team members are at each kneeler. Those coming forward are encouraged to share their concern, joy, or remain silent. They can stand, kneel, or sit on the adjacent stool.

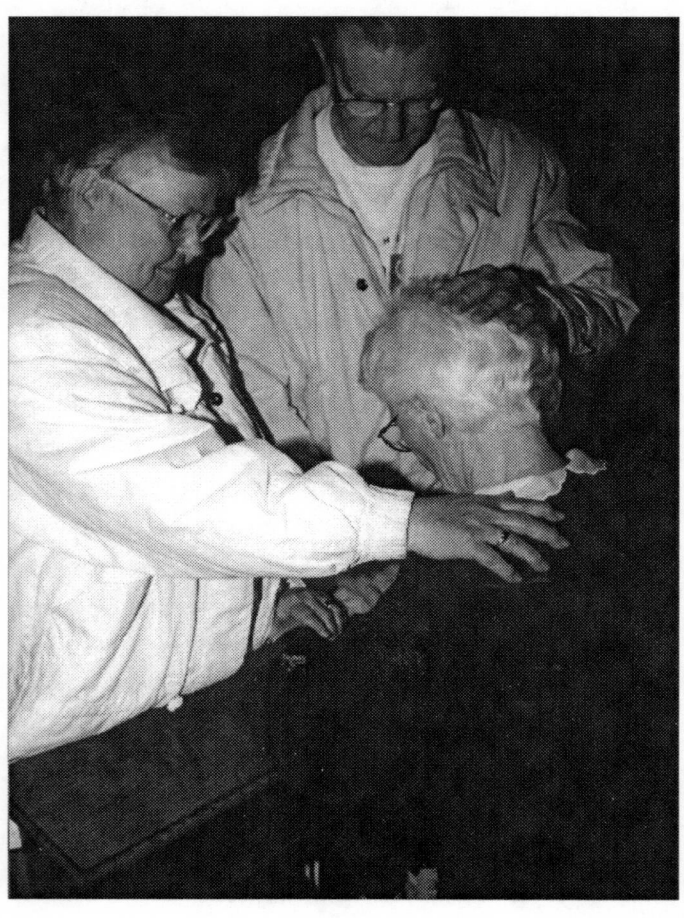

Space—It's More Than Air

Again, the prayer team follows the person's lead. Those coming forward to the kneelers are in charge. The team is the audience for their requests or silence. They let us know if we can anoint them and lay hands upon their head and shoulder. All the time Taizé music is sung, hummed, or quietly absorbed.

The person who came forward is anointed with oil by a team member and a short prayer is offered relating to the person's request. Then we pause "and rest in God's presence" for several minutes. Singing by those in the congregation and choir continues.

The second person on the team concludes with another short prayer of affirmation. Hands continue to be laid upon the shoulder or head. Often hands are being held as well. The persons who have come forward stay until they decide to leave. They have control over their "floor and space."

During this time of anointing, others in the congregation come forward to the chancel area. There they light votive candles on two large low tables. Kneeling cushions are also there. The lit candles represent prayers for particular people or causes.

The candles on the low tables begin to match the lovely votive candles placed in the reredos behind the Communion table. This service represents a new expansion of faith's dimensions.

In the darkness of a wintry early evening, those flickering candles are themselves a call to wonder and prayer. They provide another facet in the quiet space of worship.

Many who attend this one-hour service on a Saturday evening are from the community and not from the church. Several persons who have attended this service have later become a part of the congregation. A couple of them became part of the small prayer team. Training was given to those on the prayer team. That way they could begin to grasp what was taking place.

Often, when the prayer team of six-to-eight persons gather after the service, Pastor Moiso will say, "Mercy, what a privilege that we get to do this."

The prayer team is often asked to go to people's homes and share a simple time of listening and laying on of hands with prayer. Curing and healing are not usually the same thing. Healing may come in ways totally different from what was wanted. Bridges between estranged family members have been rebuilt, even though that wasn't the request in prayer.

If you want more information about the service, you'll find it in the appendix. This form of simple, quiet worship, in the midst of sometimes hectic schedules and personal needs, gives a new meaning to spiritual space.

DIFFERENT SPACE IN WORSHIP

Understanding the significance of worship and its space is important.

Space—It's More Than Air

Over the years Lenore and I have been asked to share a nonverbal clown service of Holy Communion. This is not a usual setting for two clowns, and it requires some daring on the part of a congregation.

Like any of our church-service clowning, we make sure the congregation is well informed ahead of time. Most of the usual parts of the service of worship are led by the pastor and lay leaders before the Communion service. Wrinkles and Doolotz (my tramp clown) are not seen. We are secluded, but we can hear what is happening. It is important that we are within earshot to hear our cue to enter.

Because of my background in music used in Open Door, I have been able to synchronize appropriate music for our entrance. It is from *Bela Fleck and the Flectones, "The flight of the cosmic hippo."* Once we hear the slow methodic beat, we leave the room in which we are waiting and enter the sanctuary, usually in the chancel area.

This sounds like we are "going on stage," but remember, we are the audience. The congregation is the group "on stage." Shakespeare's comment that "all the world's a stage" is most appropriate. All the sanctuary and its people are the stage. We are prepared to respond to the congregants where they are. They have been prepared to continue in worship.

Wrinkles and Doolotz are rather overwhelmed when we enter the sanctuary. We interact with people closest to where we enter. Sometimes the choir has moved into the front pews. If we know the choir director, we will pretend to direct the choir.

Wrinkles is carrying a long grocery list and oversized pencil. Doolotz has a large shopping bag on which is printed in large letters, "THE STORE." The appearance is that we've been grocery shopping.

All the time, the music that cued us to enter continues. In due time we arrive at a rather ratty looking card table with a funny tablecloth on it. There are a few pieces of table settings. These include clown mugs and candle holders of different sizes that we'll use later. Also some cloth napkins, matches, and Q-tips, plus small pill bottles with washable red face paint in them are placed on the table.

While this rather funky music is heard over the PA system, we continue to pull items from the grocery sack. Wrinkles dutifully checks them off her list as Doolotz pulls them out of the bag. All sorts of related and unrelated objects come out. A box of macaroni and cheese, a couple of candles that later go in the holders already on the table.

Out comes a plastic cottage cheese container. I smile in delight, but when I shake it, there is a questionable sound. Once opened, it is full of nails. Doolotz tests one with his teeth then checks with Wrinkles non-verbally to see if nails are on the list. She looks and shakes her head "no." Doolotz drops a few of the nails on the floor in disgust and puts the container on the table.

A narrow, flat board about two feet long is also in the sack, but Doolotz just tosses it on the ground in disgust. Wrinkles shakes her head in disbelief because it wasn't on her list either.

A couple of candles that were on Wrinkles' list appear. So Doolotz puts them into the two candleholders. After difficulty in trying to light them, he finally gets them lit. He compares their heights with the ones on the Communion table behind them. One candle is shorter than the other.

A block of wood that had been taken from the bag is used to make the two candles essentially the same height. That way, both our table and the church's Communion table will have matching candles on them, sort of.

Next, out of the bag comes the large plastic bottle of grape juice. Doolotz rubs his tummy and puts it on the card table. A long loaf of French bread appears from the sack. Doolotz motions he'd like to take a bite right then. Wrinkles vigorously shakes her head. Both of those items were on the list Wrinkles held. She dramatically checks them off.

Doolotz then looks into the sack and is astounded by what he sees. Wrinkles comes over to see what the problem is. She drops her food list and pencil in response. We both freeze in place as we look into that sack.

Bring in the Clowns—
A Metaphor for Ministry

As we wait, looking into the bag, the music segues to the very haunting music from the movie *"Chariots of Fire" - "Abraham's theme" by Vangelis.* (Polydor 1981)

Doolotz reaches carefully into the sack and pulls out a crown of thorns. He shows it to the congregation, touching the thorns and reacting. It is a crown of thorns we purchased when in Bethlehem.

Wrinkles then picks up the loaf of bread and wraps it with a large napkin. She begins to cradle it, and then lifts it up like a mother joyously holding her child aloft. She puts the "baby" on her shoulder and gently pats it.

Doolotz begins to come closer, wanting to put the crown of thorns on the "baby." Wrinkles resists as long as possible. Very reluctantly she accepts the crown of thorns as it is placed on the "baby."

While Doolotz kneels, Wrinkles slowly and deliberately tears the bread in two. This is one of the hardest moments for both of us in the service. Tears are in our eyes, and it's hard to swallow. Once having broken the bread she gently lays it on the table.

While on his knees, Doolotz finds two pieces of wood, one from the "store" and another that had been placed under the table in the set up. Taking a hammer that was on the floor already, he picks up some of the nails he had dropped from the cottage cheese container, then deliberately configures a cross. The pounding of the nails resounds in the sanctuary.

Space—It's More Than Air

Once the cross is made, Doolotz stands. Wrinkles retrieves the crown of thorns and places it over the top of the cross. It falls against the crossbeam. She removes the cap from the bottle of juice. Then lifts up the bottle so that Doolotz can take the cross and, using the cross bar, symbolically pours out the "blood of the cross" into the bottle.

Doolotz gently shakes the cross to get the last symbolic drop out of the cross. Then wipes the cross bar across the lip of the bottle. If ever there is a place where Doolotz almost loses his composure it is at this moment.

This simple but extremely moving action is from Floyd Shaffer, one of our gracious clown mentors.

Music again segues. A wide variety of prerecorded instrumental music softly plays *"Amazing Grace"* as we prepare the cups and bread for intinction. We then model what will happen for the congregation. We serve each other and place the cups and bread on the table.

As in most of our church services of worship, we again include the giving of the red dot. The congregation has been told of its significance both in printed form in the bulletin and by the persons leading worship. We are marked by the blood of Jesus' love. A spiritual baptism of identity.

Wrinkles and Doolotz model this for the congregation, each giving the other the red dot on the cheek.

Bring in the Clowns—
A Metaphor for Ministry

A small gesture brings the elders and clergy forward who are to be the ones serving the bread and unfermented wine. They station themselves at the front of the chancel steps. We often use our clown-faced mugs from our small collection.

Deacons guide people to come forward down the center aisle to the front of the chancel. After receiving the elements, the members circle around and reenter their pews from the side aisle.

Often one of the pastors and an elder are the ones offering the bread and juice. In smaller churches, elders and deacons often are at one of the stations. They will say to those receiving the elements words to the effect, "The bread of life" and "The blood of Jesus offered for you."

Meanwhile, Wrinkles and Doolotz are on opposite outside aisles offering the red dot. It can go on the cheek or the hand. Putting the dot on the cheek signifies the recipient's willingness for us to enter their personal space. Some prefer not to receive the red dot, and we honor their decision. We are the audience, they are in charge.

I remember one older woman and her husband who came my way after receiving the sacrament. The woman sort of soft-shoed her way to Doolotz, did a curtsey, smiled, and received her red dot on her cheek. Hardly what one would expect during a service of worship and especially by one of the older members. Her husband knowingly smiled as he received the red dot.

Space—It's More Than Air

But for me it became a simple reminder that this is not the sorrowful sacrament of our Lord, but the joyous reminder of what great love God has for us in his beloved Son. Yes, in our own little places we can offer back a smiling thank you to the one who gave himself in unconditional love.

Once all have been served, including elders and pastors, the elements are returned to the clowns. The elders and pastors are also given the red dot. In turn, the bread and juice are removed from our little card table and placed on the Communion table behind us. Along with the used red Q-tips, we sprinkle some of the nails upon the Communion table as well.

The funky candles of different lengths on our card table are also moved to be alongside the lovely brass candlesticks and candles on the Communion table. Looks don't really matter. The space of faith is what counts.

We then need to model one more greeting before we leave. Many of us are a bit stiff in the way we extend a greeting to another. We offer another way of modeling a greeting.

Doolotz tries to kiss Wrinkles, but our larger clown noses get in the way if we do it frontally.

After a couple of tries, Doolotz gets an "aha." He has Wrinkles throw her arms straight out. He gently tips her to her right and he can easily slip in to give her the

Bring in the Clowns—
A Metaphor for Ministry

kiss. We then hug and shake hands, which are part of the modeling of possible responses for the congregation.

Now we need to exit the sanctuary, but not before we create a little bit of chaos. We move to the persons closest to the center aisle in the first pews. We give them a hug and non-verbally urge them to pass it on. This goes on for many pews. In the meantime we've had the congregation stand and they are all hugging, kissing, and shaking hands.

The congregation continues to greet each other without our having to urge them anymore. This gives us time to slip out of the sanctuary. The music is faded, the pastor goes to the pulpit and reads this statement.

"You may ask, 'Where are the clowns?' They're already here! You have been marked with a little red dot.

Space—It's More Than Air

It symbolizes your identity with Jesus, the Son of God, who was foolish enough to give His life for us, giving us the freedom to accept his gift or to refuse it. Become 'fools for Christ' and accept his baptism of love. If you accept his baptism, say 'Amen.'"

The chaos has a conclusion. The important people again are those in the pews who were on the stage. Our focus was to provide them with emotional and spiritual space in which to fathom a tiny different approach. For some it brought a deeper meaning to the Lord's Supper.

No words were spoken by the clowns in the service. The music and actions helped us all focus on the incredible significance of the sacrament. Many of those who shared in the service were deeply moved. Along with us, tears were shared as well as laughter. The liturgy of the sacrament could be given space without a word being spoken.

A friend of ours, Bryon Garvin, is a videographer at local TV station, videotaped one of our Communion services. We always viewed that service ahead of any service we were to conduct so that we could get into that "space" in our minds and our hearts ahead of time. He made it available to us and information on borrowing the video or DVD is possible through our email address. Postage both ways is all we ask since we cannot sell the tape because we do not have the rights to the music or the video. Our email address is _budfrim@gmail.com._

Bring in the Clowns—
A Metaphor for Ministry

We remember one of the very first Communion services we shared with a church in another city. At the close of the service of worship, we slipped out and tried to stay out of sight. But one dear older woman found us. She came to us with tears in her eyes.

She said, "I've been an elder for more than thirty-five years, but I've never been so moved by Communion as I was with this. The significance of Communion spoke loudly in its silence. Thank you very much is all I can find to say."

Messages have been e-mailed to us following the service as well as beautiful encouragements. Here are a couple of their responses.

"Once again, through your wonderful clowning, you have demonstrated how much of an impact can be made without a word being spoken."

"We just want to thank you two for the wonderful Communion service on Sunday. On the way out of the sanctuary Peg said, 'That was the most meaningful Communion I have ever had,' to which I replied, 'I agree. There were tears in my eyes throughout the entire service!'"

We've been privileged to share this nonverbal clown Communion service with tiny churches, in camp settings, other denominations, overseas where our son was teaching, and even at a presbytery meeting. Words sometimes get in the way of deeply significant experiences. We just have to smile and move on with lumps

in our throats, but alleluias in our hearts. I think God
accepts that kind of response.

> That little piece of bread
>> The tiny sip of juice
>> So small in size
>> Yet immense in significance
>> Whether it be from the hands
>>> of priests or pastors
>>> elders or deacons
>>> male or female
>> Ageless is its meaning
>> Leading us beyond this moment—
>> For with every meal we share
>> Being one person or many
>> That moment also becomes the opportunity
>> To "do this in remembrance of me."
>> Gracious God, thank you for remembering us.

LETTING THE SPACE AROUND YOU SPEAK

Often people say that being in a natural setting
with a spacious view gives them a sense of awe. Distant
mountains, frothy streams, stunning sunsets or sunrises,
thunder and bolts of lightning shattering the skies are
awe-filled. In what way do these "spacial" experiences
touch and move you?

Our son Todd teaches in elementary schools. He has
often had his class (and their parents if they choose) go
to a local park early in the morning. Sitting on a hillside,

they may be sipping hot cocoa or coffee and chewing on a bagel. He has those present write about what they experience as the sun rises. Charming, thoughtful, humorous, and sensitive writings come from both students and parents.

They are all in the same "space," but their experiences are vastly different. Why not try this yourself? You don't need to get up early, unless that's a comfortable thing to do. Catch the sunrise or a sunset. Let the words flow without worrying about meter or rhyme. Pour out your thoughts.

I often visualize prose while viewing space around me. What I have experienced lets my spirit tie in with the one whose dimensions are unlimited. If I have my camera, I will catch that moment on film. Later, I let the prose I felt when I saw the sight roll on paper and then attach the photo with it.

One of these days I'll do something more with the stack of more than 300 photos and prose. They are together on a table, not yet well organized into some kind of meaningful system. But I need to give myself the space of time to let that process happen.

Try similar things with music, pieces of art, or how some music has lifted you beyond the moment; all is special space. You'll continue to be awed that it's more than air.

We learn from these experiences as clowns, teachers, pastors, or others in ministry. Space is very important to each of us. Perhaps we begin to realize how very labor intensive ministry becomes.

Time and effort, listening and sensing the other persons require intentional work. But in the process we gain insight and inspiration from those around us. The breath of the Spirit moves wherever it pleases. When we catch a wisp of that movement in our lives, we are changed. Once we realize this, we move on.

As Dennis Benson reminded me, "Welcome to the desert where you'll discover two abiding things: you are called to be faithful, and you will never be alone." In that space you are given opportunity to continue growing.

QUESTIONS FOR MORE REFLECTIONS

1. Recall those times when the sacrament of the Lord's Supper touched you in ways you hadn't experienced before. What was the occasion? Who was involved? In what way was this different from other services? Were you allowed to discover the space? Or did you take time to find the "space" to reflect on what happened? How has that affected you when you have received the elements since that time?

2. If you are clergy or designated persons who lead the service of worship, what kinds of preparations do you make? I remember a young teenage girl who came into the kitchen where the elements for Communion were being prepared.

Bring in the Clowns—
A Metaphor for Ministry

Her comment was, "Oh goody. Refreshments!" Does that offend you, or does it bring another depth to your understanding of the Lord's Supper as a time for spiritual refreshment and profound joy?

3. What kinds of experiences have you had in dealing with spatial concerns? We call the sanctuary a holy place or holy space. How do you respond to the sanctuary when you enter it for worship? Is it a time for closing the spaces with others whom you have not seen for awhile? How do you prepare yourself when you enter this special room? Are there other rooms that provide you with this sense of special space?

4. Take some moments to recall places and times when you have discovered that someone has given you a "spatial moment." It may be in a specific juncture in your life. You may recall when you have offered to others a "spatial moment" and sense what it meant to be able to share it.

5. Where do you see the tie-in of space and knowing who the audience is as you lead a discussion or offer words of encouragement? If a clergy person, how has the space you discover in your relationships with your congregants made your ministry more meaningful? It may come in the winsome smile of parishioners as they leave worship.

Space—It's More Than Air

In memorial services it is quite common for an "open mike" experience to happen. People relate how the person who had died has given them a new breadth of understanding. If people spoke about you after you have died, what would they have to say about you? What would you like them to know? Would space be one of your gifts to them? Could you share that with them before they died?

6. How willing would you be to have clowns share in worship, especially in the sacraments of baptism or the Lord's Supper? Are you able to include sacred dance? We recently had a short piece of sacred dance along with a mime to offer another view of Pentecost while our choir sang an appropriate anthem. The woman sitting next to us in the pew said, "I just hate it when things like this happen." It was out of her "space" of convenience and understanding. Can you relate to her spatial needs?

Is it too daring to offer these approaches? Reflect on special services of worship in which you have participated. What are some of the strong memories they have produced for you? How comfortable are you as a layperson, clergy, or clown to suggest variations in how to use the space in worship? How would you respond

Bring in the Clowns—
A Metaphor for Ministry

to some approaches that you found quite daring and different? How can you measure what is appropriate?

Space is more than just air. It is a means of protecting yourself and a way of exploring God's gracious world.

Chapter 7

Profound Simplicity
or Chaos

For nearly twenty-one years I was privileged to produce a nationally and internationally distributed radio program called Open Door. Since the studios where the thirty-minute program was produced were in use during the day time, we had to switch to night use. That process, plus having to originally work at both a pastoral ministry and Open Door, made me into more of a night person.

This could have caused difficulties in a marriage relationship if it weren't for an extremely supportive wife. I worked at 62KGW from roughly 5:00 in the evening until the wee hours in the morning of the next day. I did this two days a week. On Wednesdays I would have breakfast with Lenore, but wouldn't again see her face in daylight hours until Friday supper.

Bring in the Clowns—
A Metaphor for Ministry

We'd share the same bed, only I wouldn't get into it until 2:00 or 3:00 A.M. As a consequence, she rose at dawn, had breakfast, and went to work at SOAR, the acronym for Sponsors Organized to Assist Refugees. This was the refugee office where she worked. When she arrived home on both Wednesday and Thursday evening after work I was already at the radio station. It was a workable solution, but required a great deal of trust and overwhelming love.

Talk about a potentially explosive marital problem that never happened. Her biggest concern on many nights was when it was very late and she had awakened to find I wasn't home yet. Usually I'd call her earlier in the evening during a break in the recording sessions at the station to check on her day. However, when the clock revealed midnight and beyond, I didn't want to disturb her sleep.

Some evenings, especially when winter struck and the roads could be snowy or icy, she would call me at the station. I had to drive over pretty-good-sized hills that top the west side of Portland. That area often became treacherous. She wanted to make sure I would make it home all in one piece. Lenore's concern was what I call a sense of profound love. It was as simple as that.

This same pattern we set in our working days follows us into retirement. I no longer go to the station or to regular pastoral work. But I learned that I often do my best thinking as the evening becomes later. After watching the late TV news and a bit of late shows for a few laughs, we finally make our way to bed.

KINK-fm is a local radio station that had helped Open Door by allowing us to use some of their music albums for the program. It was also a sister station in the same building with 62KGW. They have a late-night program called "Lights Out." Its quiet, reflective music is aired from 10:00 P.M. to midnight. Commercials are usually heard only at the top of the two hours of music. We find it a great way to slip quietly into sleep, because my radio has a timer that we can set to turn it off.

But I'm not always quite ready for sleep. So when the commercials come on at midnight, I'll reach over to our little clock radio and click over to KOAP-fm, the local NPR station. They have BBC radio news at the top of the hour. At the stroke of midnight I get the very latest from England. It's 7:00 A.M., Greenwich Mean Time, and another part of the world is awakening as I prepare to snooze.

The five-minute newscast gave me the latest news that was breaking in that part of the world as their day began. You can tell I'm sort of a news junkie to want that kind of information after the quiet music!

One night as they closed down the newscast, I was about to turn the radio off, but they mentioned something about clowns. My interest allowed me to give up a few moments of needed rest. I wanted to know what they were going to say.

Bring in the Clowns—
A Metaphor for Ministry

They used some old Spike Jones madcap music to segue into their little program bits. What I discovered was that they were talking about a different kind of clown than what Wrinkles and Doolotz are. Under discussion were all the little tricks and put downs that clowns give to each other and sometimes to their audiences.

It was evident they were entertainers. One word they used again and again was that their kind of clowning needed to be at the level of "stupidity." One of them said words to the effect that the only way you could be a clown was to be stupid enough to have a shaving cream pie smashed into your face. That was to give the audience a laugh.

Lenore and I have never thrown a pie in anyone's face, a clown or straight person. Nor have we thought about it, although many people expect to see clowns do such "stupid" tricks.

But those entertaining clowns are not stupid. They plan their gigs very well to achieve maximum laughter. The idea that seemed to be presented was that to be childlike you had to be somewhat stupid.

Maybe it was the word "stupid" that bothered me. That's a real put down whether you think of it yourself or lay it on another. "That's a stupid mistake." or "He certainly managed to be stupid instead of using his best ideas." Stupid is such a negative feeling word that it rattled me, especially as they spoke of clowns needing to be stupid!

Profound Simplicity or Chaos

I'd rather think of clowning, and for that matter most forms of ministry, as simple. Involved, yes. Maybe a bit complicated, but still having the ability to see more clearly what is happening. Perhaps we can relate to what Thomas Merton called "the silence printed in our being."

Silent simplicity. Profound simplicity. My thesaurus refers to simplicity as being modest, plain, innocent, guileless, natural, unpretentious, plus a few more. But that doesn't strike to the center of my comprehension for what simplicity means.

Perhaps the experience I had standing in St. Peter's Cathedral in the Vatican will help. Lenore and I were with a group in the early 1970s that traveled to both Israel and Rome, Italy. The size and splendor of that cathedral still causes deep awe for me, especially as I'm reminded of it every day. We have a large copy of Michelangelo's "Creation of Man" from the Sistine Chapel hanging in our living room.

But I was most struck with profound empathy standing in front of the Pieta, the exquisite sculptures of Mary cradling her slain son Jesus across her lap. It is a magnificent sculpture that speaks to me even as I type these words. I was fortunate enough at that time to have a clear path to the statues and have a very moving photograph I took of the scene. The statues have now been encased in shatterproof glass, because someone tried to destroy the figures. But earlier I had a clear path for the picture.

Bring in the Clowns–
A Metaphor for Ministry

From that photo, I was moved to write these words:

PROFOUND PIETY -
        INCREDIBLE PIETA

SUCH WORKS BY MASTERS OF OLD
TAKE SIMPLICITY TO ITS ULTIMATE
        DEPTH
AND THERE PARTIALLY FATHOM
       WHAT TOOK PLACE
        WHAT TAKES PLACE
WHENEVER YOU STOP FOR A MOMENT
    AND DISCOVER
        MILLENNIA

How often in our experiences as both clowns and people in ministry, we discover profound simplicity. It could be in the work of a Stephen Minister, a layperson who is trained to actively listen, sitting by the bed of sick persons holding their hand. Or that engaging smile and laughter of a child whose mental capabilities are limited but responds to the sounds of a clown's little plastic siren.

You discover this in gentle touches of understanding when reaching out to a person who has suffered the loss of a loved one. Hugs are those incredibly personal ways of exchanging loving thoughts without a word. Or the slowly running tear of a child who has a tiny bump, but is lovingly kissed and held by her mother.

Somehow we get caught up in thinking we need to do extraordinary things to accomplish mission and

Bring in the Clowns—
A Metaphor for Ministry

ministry. People like Mother Teresa remind us that, "We may not be able to do great things, but we can do things with great love."

The Scriptures are filled with moments when simple actions change a whole attitude. Take the woman at the well when Jesus met her there. The disciples had gone into town for supplies. Here came the woman at noontime, not the usual time for drawing water from this ancient well. She was an outcast because her life was rather shady, even to this moment. The other village women would have come for water early in the morning, possibly talking about "that certain woman" in the village.

Jesus had other eyes with which to see a person. He made a simple request for a drink of water on a warm day. He crossed over many rivers of stormy prejudices with his request. First, he was talking to a woman at a well, often the meeting place for romance. He also knew all about her shady past and present. Yet, he talked with her.

Besides, men didn't usually talk to women in a public place. She also knew their cultures were different. She was a Samaritan and he a Jew; those two cultures didn't even speak to each other. But Jesus did.

She marveled that he knew so much about her and yet accepted her as a person of value. The Scriptures of John 4 give a perceptive description of how Jesus accepted people for who they were. Like the imprint that

Profound Simplicity or Chaos

Merton wrote about, Jesus also challenged listeners by his acceptance, to become more of what God intended.

The woman dropped her "bucket" and rushed into town. Her testimony was so convincing that the townsfolk ran to see this man at the well. A shady lady became one of the earliest evangelists for Jesus, all because of that meeting where Jesus asked for a drink of water.

Pastors can develop many ideas from that text for sermons. Lenore and I have shared it in pantomime. I rewrote the passage a little bit and she acted it out. She came dressed close to what we imagined the woman would be wearing. She also came carrying a metal pail; we didn't have a large jar. That way we wouldn't have to worry about dropping a clay jar and breaking it on the sanctuary floor. When she dropped an unbiblical metal bucket on the floor, its sound only made her running down the center aisle more dramatic. She had a mission. As the woman at the well, she was to share the good news of accepting love with the whole community.

If you should be desperate for more information on such little dramatizations of Scripture, I have included a few in the appendix. The point of this is to remind us all that sometimes the most innocent, genuine actions can produce powerful responses.

Dr. Patch Adams takes other caring clowns with him to dangerous places in this world. People pay for the privilege of going to Bosnia, Israel, Palestine, or Southeast Asia. There, with the awesome gifts of gentle humor, balloons, smiles, and gentle touches, people respond. Language is no barrier to natural gifting. In most cases, those who thought they were giving were the recipients of deeply-moving experiences.

PUTTING SIMPLICITY INTO "BEING"

Being genuine can be both difficult and yet simple. In the VOCA camp, finding a buddy who will listen to all of one's babbling without being hit and told to "shut up" is unbelievable when the opposite is what the child has only known. To have a safe place even for a few days makes anyone realize that living this way is possible.

Like so many simple gifts, what is discovered is genuine hope. Hope that my life can change. Encouragement that I am a person of worth. Trust that I can continue to mature and be a dispenser of caring love. Anticipate that the memories of past abuse will be outlasted by experiences that make us realize that "the sunshine starts here!" inside of us.

Wrinkles and Zyppurr met a pleasant man in the room where I had been for my heart surgery. He was probably in his early 50s. As he allowed us into his room, he mentioned, "You visited me five years ago when I was here."

He said this with a smile of appreciation. "And you're still doing it!"

Usually when persons say they have seen us before, we need to change the shtick. I have little tray favors with small origami peace birds pasted in one corner of the card. This is what is written on the rest of the favor:

Profound Simplicity or Chaos

WE'VE SHARED A MOMENT WITH YOU
BEFORE
MAY THIS PEACE BIRD OF HOPE REMIND
YOU
THAT YOU'RE NEVER ALL ALONE.

I asked him if he knew the story of 1,000 peace birds. We call them peace birds, but they are really cranes. Since he didn't know the story, we told him an abbreviated version of the story.

A young girl in Hiroshima was affected by the radiation from the atomic bomb. It took a while before her illness was diagnosed. A traditional Japanese story is that if you made 1,000 origami peace cranes while you were sick, you would become well. The little child didn't make it to 600 before she died.

However, the community did not forget her. Today there is a lovely, tall metal structure with 1,000 peace cranes in homage to this little child and for the principle of peace.

When I had my heart bypass surgery, Lisa, the 11-year-old daughter of Sharyn Hedbloom, started making them for me. She and another girl her age folded 1,000 tiny peace cranes and gave them to me for Christmas a short time after my surgery.

During my recovery, while we were making our plans to take clowning to the cardiac ward, we thought of the peace birds. So now when we travel the halls of the hospital and come to persons we've seen before, we offer the little tray favor with a colorful tiny peace bird in the corner.

As persons in ministry—lay, clergy, and even clowns—there are times when the simplest word or action brings the greatest and most memorable moments.

I remember being in the ER as a clergyman with a dear friend and her family. The family had asked me to be with them. They were told there was nothing further that could be done for their beloved mother. She had become brain-dead. The option before them was to either sustain her life artificially or have those mechanical devices turned off.

We gathered around her bed and held hands or put them lovingly upon her wasted body. Brief prayers were shared by family, and they asked me to give the blessing and benediction as the machines were turned off.

She escaped our little view of life in those precious moments. She who had been a sensitive mentor of her family had physically left us. But her wonderful smile was etched deeply in our minds. Her Oklahoman wit and slight southern accent would ever be with us. So much so that I can visualize her smile and hear her saying, "Hello, Bud."

"Hang on to Christ and in all else hang loose."

That phrase has helped me through many a fire. It's really my version of a statement used by a distinguished Anglican pastor. Dr. Leslie Weatherhead quoted it more completely in his book *The Christian Agnostic* (Abingdon Press 1965). Dr. Herbert Butterfield wrote: "Hold to Christ and for the rest be totally uncommitted" (*Christianity and History*).

I remember my version a little easier. It was a short statement that still rings true to me forty years later. It is a mantra, if you please, of how I look at ministry, how I approach clowning, and how I am as an individual. No one is more important to me than Jesus the Christ. He reveals who God is both in action and word.

This allows me to follow the words of another insightful poet who urges us "to live the questions." We can't put God in a box. All too many of us have tried to put God there, only to discover that God is much too large for our little theories and concepts. Yahweh is a word Jews won't speak, a name we translate in a wide variety of ways, but really can't grasp. God is more than we can formalize or theorize.

"Hanging loose" is my hook, because it means I've made a commitment to the person who is my Lord, Master, Savior, and daily friend.

What could be more direct or unpretentious than Jesus' call for us "to love one another as I have loved you"? Yet, how powerful. His words grab me. I know that I fail to express or even own up to that love when I'm challenged in my faith. Yet God doesn't stop loving me. "Jesus loves me this I know, for the Bible tells me so!" No wonder Karl Barth quoted those words in response to a question about a simple statement of faith. Who am I to differ?

All of which is an assumption. Life is a long series of assumptions. Either God *is* or *is not*. Either Jesus is Lord of my life, or he is not. Either my wife believes that I love her, or she doesn't. Fortunately, for more than fifty years she continues to tell me it is so. Believe me, it is with deep gratitude that I accept her love.

Where can we as clowns express this love? Wrinkles carries with her little colorful 2"x4" slips of paper. Printed on them is a cute little teddy bear. Underneath the bear are these words:

Free Hug Certificate
Claim Anytime
Reusable

We give these hug certificates to just about every person we meet in the hospital: patients, family members, hospital staff, construction workers. They receive them with a smile and sometimes a hug right then and there to Wrinkles.

But we also know that on 2G, my old cardiac ward, nurses, aides, and staff people will respond with hugs when a patient asks for them. In fact, at one time we saw one of our hug certificates posted on the nurses' bulletin board. They also had a little statement encouraging the sharing of hugs when a patient asked for one. It reminded them that hugs don't cost any money, but give the patient a tiny moment of encouragement.

Profound Simplicity or Chaos

Our friend Shobi Dobi, in one of her quarterly Hospital Clown newsletters, wrote of clowns following the 9/11 strike in New York City. Caring clowns came to the scene as rescue workers, trauma workers, police, and firemen dealt with the crisis.

They weren't even sure they could get close to the tragedy since the area was blocked off. Somehow, when those working at that terrible tragedy saw the clowns, they found relief. Many received clown hug certificates and immediately claimed them from the clowns.

Police and firemen were seen wearing red sponge noses. It was in a totally obscene terrorist action that the light of hope was given. A fireman or rescue worker with a red nose reminded all that love would win. Simple, daring actions by complete outsiders, silly old caring clowns, lifted spirits by genuine acts of grace, red sponge noses, and hugs.

QUIET SIMPLICITY IN THE COMMON EXPERIENCES

We have a cozy back yard where we live. It's just large enough to have two fair-sized fig trees of different varieties, a lovely flowering Japanese cherry, and a dogwood whose blossoms in the spring make a blur of white, each blossom in the shape of a cross. I've taken many pictures of their blossoms often against a brilliant azure sky.

Along the back fence I have some roses that I dearly love with fancy and exciting names. Some even have

Bring in the Clowns— A Metaphor for Ministry

luscious, perfumed smells. A grouping of miniature roses is in the front of the beds. We use them as gifts on Sunday mornings at worship. They come in a variety of colors and shades.

Over the years we have found little coat lapel vases in which we usually put two miniature roses. Behind our lapels are straight pins. When we meet new persons in worship, we greet them. Often they observe our roses, which is a great clue for us to act. We then offer them each a rose and a pin for their lapels.

One young couple we greeted this way was most gracious. About a year after they had become members of Westminster Presbyterian Church, Dan and Mimi Burkholder approached me during the coffee hour.

"A relative of ours has been a florist and is cleaning out some of his supplies. He asked if we knew anyone who could use miniature rose vases. Would you like them?"

What an appropriate gift. The box held over 100 clear-glass vases, just the size for the tiny roses we share. They are slender and rather handsome. So now we have added giving the vases with the roses. Our pockets jingle a bit as both Lenore and I carry two in our pockets. But the sound is a delightful reminder of our opportunity to do a simple act of sharing! In fact, we have used all of them and many homes have their tiny gift to use again and again.

We had not planned to share the roses when we first planted them, but when we found the lapel vases, the next step was easy to take. Responses from couples or separate individuals were encouraging. What happened in church has brought us into contact with strangers whom we could welcome. Some have said many years later, how "inviting" it was to be welcomed in this way.

But other activities in our backyard remind me of the singleness of simplicity. Several times a day I'll go into our garage and load up some old plastic yogurt and cottage cheese containers. They're filled with sunflower, nyjer, and millet seeds along with a dried corn cob.

Having rather low-slung fig and cherry trees makes it easy to drop off sunflower seeds on their larger lower branches. At the east end of our little yard is a much larger corkscrew black locust tree. One long branch reaches way out from about two feet off the ground. We've had an arborist put a strong metal wire to anchor the branch to the trunk farther up. This was to maintain that branch so it wouldn't break off.

This is the second "feeding tree." I'll sprinkle all three kinds of seeds on the bulging limb with lots of gnarly burls. The bark is course with many wonderful places for the seeds to slip into, giving the birds and squirrels some additional work to find them.

We also have hung bird feeders with a squirrel inhibiter on the post where they are hung. Some six squirrels regularly make their appearance in their search for food. They often try to climb the pole on which the other feeders for small birds are hung. But the inverted half bell-shaped device stops them every time.

As you can tell, our "recreation" money is spent on keeping these little creatures happy. Our bedroom windows are within six feet of the large locust tree. As I've mentioned earlier, I'm essentially a night person, but the squirrels aren't.

Often in the morning, long before I've awakened, several squirrels will chatter outside our window. They're in the tree wondering when breakfast will be served! It is a little irritating, but a reminder of the extent of their dependence upon us.

Now let me make it clear, these little creatures have many places in our neighborhood to search for food. They have other natural sources as well. We happen to be one more place where they climb the trees and wires to visit. So when I hear them out there on the tree, I will sometimes grudgingly get up and go to the garage to get some food.

With my slippers on, I step out onto our deck and easily toss several handfuls of seeds toward the tree. They get their early-morning snack, and I get an early wake-up call. But since I'm retired, I can slip back in for a few more moments of shuteye, or turn on NPR for "Morning Edition" and the news. Often it hasn't changed much from the midnight version, but has longer segments.

Many people know that these little squirrels can become somewhat tame as they learn to trust us. We had one we called "Sweetie" that came daily to our sliding

Profound Simplicity or Chaos

patio door. We have a long galley kitchen with a dining room area. Our patio door is right next to where we have our meals.

Sweetie came looking in our patio door while we were sitting there looking at her. A friend told us that squirrels like peanut butter, so we found some wooden Popsicle sticks, dabbed a chunk of peanut butter on one, and offered it to Sweetie.

It wasn't love at first sight for her to be brave enough to accept our offering. But as she came more often to nibble on the sunflower seeds we had in a little pan by the patio, she was less afraid. Little by little she came to trust us. We'd pass a little stick of peanut butter through the slightly opened patio door. Her tiny paws would quickly grab it, then she'd turn and go a few feet away and nibble on it. She often licked it completely clean.

Bring in the Clowns—
A Metaphor for Ministry

Ultimately, she would almost want to come into our house. But that was one gift we simply would not allow. Imagine what a mess that would be if she had full range of a house!

Unfortunately a few months later we found her impaled on a wire fence and had the local animal rescue people take her body away. We were saddened by the loss and wondered if that would be the end of our little feeding experience. A few months later another little squirrel became adventurous; thus, the friendship continues.

I often have reflective times with these birds and squirrels. I feel quite protective of them, especially when I see a certain large black-and-white cat.

I have no ill feelings about cats except those that chase my little creatures in our back yard. That black-and-white creature can see me approaching the patio door on the inside and will scoot away. It knows that a "mean old man" doesn't appreciate its presence.

Portland generally has fairly mild winters. We may have snow for a week or two, plenty of cold and freezing weather, and sometimes ice. But somehow, I try to make sure that these creatures are fed.

Anna Hummingbirds are year-round creatures in Portland. In winter I keep changing the feeders for them. One feeder is always in the garage where it won't freeze and I can exchange it with the frozen one. Those tiny birds dart right up to our house where the feeder is located.

Profound Simplicity or Chaos

I can stand at the patio door and look eyeball to eyeball with them, about eighteen inches away. A nephew of ours, Scott Burns, who lived in the mountains of Colorado had humming birds he was even able to pet as they fed. That's something I haven't tried.

These creatures remind me of the relationship we have with our Creator. I like to keep the little creatures fed. Their antics bring great joy to both Lenore and me. While we don't actually touch one another directly, we are "in touch" and often are quite close.

Read the classic poetry of Psalm 104 and see God's delight in the creatures. I especially enjoy verse 26 where it speaks of "Leviathan that you formed to sport" in the sea—living creatures to enjoy just as they are.

Jesus encouraged his disciples to love one another as he loved them. He knew that love would give them the food their spirits needed. As Dennis reminded me again and again, "Bud, you're not alone. Nothing can separate you from the love of God." You can depend upon God.

These little backyard creatures have taught me that lesson almost in reverse. While they are capable of looking for food in other places, they honor us by returning again and again. Their thanks are to be a part of our aging family. No words are exchanged, even though we talk to them!

There seems to be something between us. After all, we all are creatures with different abilities and gifts. We're part of a plan that is beyond us, but with us all of our lives. The Creator loves us. How our aching world needs to accept that love in place of hatred and greed.

If you are a clown or in some other form of ministry, professional or lay, take time to watch the animals. They may not speak our language, but you can learn from them. Remember that Jesus spoke of how God loves the lowly sparrow; not one falls without God's awareness.

That overwhelms me when I read those words. But then I remember a slip of an idea. Maybe, just maybe, those little creatures in our back yard know that, too. I don't want to harm them, just provide food and a loving place for them. My little sharing of some nibbles is a tiny reflection of the cosmos' idea of how God looks upon us. I certainly hope so.

Maybe it's that profoundly simple.

SERENDIPITIES PROVIDE OPPORTUNITIES
FOR SIMPLICITY

One of the clowns with whom we have shared our "fun shops" is John Larsen. A retired schoolteacher, John discovered clowning later in life. He is what one would call a "natural." A great deal of empathy courses through his presence, not only as a clown, but also in other circumstances.

Each year we have been asked to provide clowns at a fund-raising event for the Providence Child Center for Medically Fragile Children. It's a three-day event called "The Festival of the Trees." Various groups decorate elaborate settings for Christmas trees. Those decorations are then sold as a money raiser for the Child Center. John has been to a number of these festivals just before Christmas.

One year, he learned they needed to have volunteers to act as Santa Claus. They would greet children and go through the usual bit of asking children what they wanted for Christmas. Then a photo was made of the child with Santa. John said he always wanted to play Santa Claus, so he got the volunteer gig.

He worked not only the several hours as Santa, but also had spent two hours as "Runamuck the Clown" before changing costumes. Being the caring person that he is as a teacher, clown, and Santa, this extending of himself was no big deal. He loved it. John also shared one of his serendipitous experiences with us.

"While getting the privilege to be Santa at the Festival of Trees last year, I noticed what seemed like a family cluster in the line to see me. Perhaps a grandpa and his middle-aged children. Most likely the group included a small child I couldn't see, a child who wanted to see Santa.

"They waited their turn, and occasionally I could see the older man jumping up and down, eyes flashing in excitement. Nope, this visit was for him. The next generation down from the older man waited very supportively with him, like any responsible adults would do with someone who wanted to see Santa. The family showed no embarrassment about a grown-up man wanting to see Santa. I thought, 'God put the right folks with him.'

"His walk up to see Santa was bouncy. I hoped he didn't expect to sit on Santa's lap. He sat next to me. His eyes sparkled. He was unable to sit still. I asked him what he wanted for Christmas this year, and he rushed to tell me.

"His family or caregivers hadn't intruded on his time with Santa, and I sort of wished they had been able to eavesdrop so they could have made sure his wish came true. Then it occurred to me that maybe people who had gifted him with their support and care would be sure that Santa brought him something he wanted.

"He said goodbye, got his candy cane from a thoughtful Santa's helper, and left. He came back three times later that afternoon with his family, just to peek over the dividers, smile, and wave at Santa.

"I was hoping the man was going to get his Christmas wish, but he unknowingly had given me a precious gift, a chance to think about how awesome it would be if adults could step out of their expected roles to believe unquestioningly, to have their whole body come alive with happiness and faith. Months later, I realize that we've been given exactly that chance by God's gift to us at Christmas."

John has offered another gift to others; he has begun his newest journey as a therapeutic caring clown at the Portland Providence hospital, the place where we've clowned for ten years. He has taken a strong hold on

Profound Simplicity or Chaos

the meaning of profound simplicity at the hospital as "Doc Runamuck the Clown."

Bring in the Clowns—
A Metaphor for Ministry

QUESTIONS FOR REFLECTION

1. Dr. Howard Thurman was a captivating preacher and sensitive pastor. In one of his sermons he mentioned seeing a tire beside the road. He went and examined it, because it looked really good. However, when he nudged it, the tire crumbled a bit inside. It looked good, but it was a deception. He asked why. He learned that it had no elasticity.

    This raises the question about those of us given the Good News to share. How much elasticity do you have? Are you a type "A" personality where everything has to be in place, done decently and in order? What values are there in that position, because there certainly are some? What if you were too flexible? How does that effect what you do? Clowns can have routines that have definite directions in order to get a laugh; but do they often become "on stage" and forget who really is the audience?

2. Check your memory banks for those profound photographs that have moved you. Those awesome photos from 9/11, the raising of the flag on Iwo Jima, "Mission Accomplished" on the deck of an aircraft carrier, Mother Teresa laying her hands on an outcast, the fireman holding a wounded child in the Oklahoma City bombing. Recall pictures of a child or of a loved one who

has died that have moved you. Remember a picture that has profoundly affected you. It may not be nationally known, but brings incredible remembrances to mind.

3. Think of experiences that have been most simple, but are memorable. The arthritic, gnarled hands of an older person, words of a poem or a short saying that have affected your life. Lasting music from great composers, or the simple playing of "Chop Sticks" brings back a bundle of remembrances. Recall a time when the bread and wine were served to you in a way that brings a lump in your throat.

4. Take time to jot down ideas on slips of paper that suggest something beyond what you normally think. Place them in a pocket of your clothing hanging in the closet to be discovered another time.

5. Why is it that we have so much trouble of "not really getting it" when Jesus calls us to love one another as he has loved us? What kind of prose would you write to release that thought in new ways for yourself?

   As a clown, remember a moment when love was shared with you in a way that will always touch you. Recall when someone offered deep appreciation for your tender antics, either by words or by a most gracious smile, or a welcome hug.

Bring in the Clowns—
A Metaphor for Ministry

6. At VOCA camp, a young camper responded to her buddy by saying, "Nobody listens to me... but you did!" Simply listening.

Where do you know you've been heard? That doesn't always mean there needs to be a response from the other person. Just being truly understood is a life-preserving gift. Let your memory banks select some of those significant moments. Make sure you remember they are there to be cashed in when needed. But they'll still be there to be spent time and time again.

Chapter 8

After The Gig
or
Evaluating Your Ministry

One of the most important reminders you can provide yourself is an evaluation of the most recent event. When we have finished with our afternoon of hospital clowning, we go to our "Read all about it" notebook. In it we have recorded incidents that seemed to matter. Some of those you have read earlier in this book.

For a number of years we used a little hand-held tape recorder to catch the memory of the moment. We would leave the main hospital and sit in our car. It must have been an interesting sight for anyone who was parked next to us. Two old clowns in their fourteen-year-old car talking into a small hand-held dictating recorder.

We later transferred the comments into our little book. It also has become a place to put in pictures from events with which we have helped. This kind of evaluation is important, because it serves two purposes. First, it is good for recall of what part of the clowning that was effective. Secondly, the record of the event gives us insights into how to better reach patients, their families, and staff. We have been able to change some of our approaches for another time.

In other forms of ministry, this same recording of what happened is important. I found it most helpful to keep records of calls that I made, and to include little reminders of what happened. Sometimes it included the name of their family pet or persons in the household. This greatly assisted my memory.

Keeping a diary was most helpful when calling upon a family whom we hadn't seen in some time. To be aware of their comments from previous contacts helps to relieve a bit of the tension. Rather than saying, "Why haven't we seen you in church lately?" which puts them on the defensive, you can say something like, "We've missed you. Have you been ill and we didn't know it?"

My wife made these kinds of calls on people who haven't seen in worship lately at the church we attend. In the process, she discovered that one person wasn't at home when Lenore called. She was caring for her mother in a town close by. Her mother was in the late stages of hospice care.

That gave the pastoral staff an opportunity to contact the woman in the new location. She wasn't angry with the church. She just had an important responsibility. The pastors needed to know that information and make a personal call.

I realize this seems like just another thing for pastors to do. But if we are concerned about those with whom we share ministry, a few minutes of recording information can be helpful. With all the recent electronic means of doing such recording, this can be a simple task. As one who served most of my pastoral ministry in small churches, even the pen and 3"x5" card file served me well. My memory wasn't always accurate in recalling some of the important nuances that related to families.

How This Relates To Vocation

Through these pages I've shared some of the ways in which my calling has been a challenge. Earlier I wrote about that inner voice that said, "Trust me." It was a call to go in a new direction. Take the risk. "Go for it!" has become a favorite statement with which Lenore often challenges me.

Look at Matthew 14:22-33. Jesus is walking on water. Peter wants to have the same experience and steps out of the boat. He manages a few steps, then falters when the wind begins to pick up. Jesus reaches out and helps him get back in the boat.

We might fault Peter for his lack of faith, but he did make the effort. He "went for it" and found out quickly that he wasn't up to that event. The important experience was that he gave it a "go." He failed at fulfilling what he expected, but Jesus rescued him. The effort was there. The execution was not completed because he was afraid.

We're not called to walk on water, even if we know where the big rocks are just below the surface. But we are called upon to take the risk. Peter later became the number-one disciple and led the early church even to his martyrdom

"Taking the plunge" is one of the steps in vocation. Sometimes it leads to hard places where we are risking "what is" for "what can be." I discovered that when I left the comforting financial womb of pastoring a church. My calling was in another place.

At the time of that voice saying "Trust me," we had a house mortgage to pay and our three young adults were in private colleges. My church salary in 1979 was around $25,000 including pension, housing, car allowance, and medical benefits.

The Open Door board offered me $10,000 total for the same package! At least a $15,000 drop in income. Lenore said she'd go to work and, as I've written earlier, she found her calling. At first it was part time, but became full time for almost thirteen years.

With that entire financial burden, I had to have the courage. I'm usually not a bold person to follow that inner voice. It's a good thing I didn't consult a vocational expert or a psychiatrist at that time. No financial advisor would have had a thing to do with me.

"Trust me" happened in 1979, yet that call still seems to be pertinent in retirement. Ministry never really ends for any of us whom Christ has called. In 2 Peter 1:10 are these words: "Make God's call and His choice of you a permanent experience" (*Good News translation*). Being willing to extend yourself is the clue to both clowning and other forms of ministry.

My calling is no different from anyone else's. The circumstances and challenges simply have different names. Vocation always carries with it the sense of risk. Is it right for me, for now? Is this the direction I need to use the gifts God has given me? What are my best gifts, and how does God want me to use them?

In a recent conversation with Todd, our teacher son, he related something that gives a bit of direction. He has been teaching in elementary and middle school settings here in the States and in Riyadh, Saudi Arabia, Hong Kong, and Vienna, Austria. He knows about travel, risk, and what it has done for his young family.

Todd related taking a special inventory that checked out his interests and abilities. I asked him to relay that information to me from Vienna.

He wrote, "It's called the 'theory of multiple intelligences.' There are currently nine identified." (In the Appendix you will find the web sites he used.)

Bring in the Clowns—
A Metaphor for Ministry

Through the results of this inventory that he found online, one particular interest surprised him. His strongest interest was in music. It startled him to realize this quality until he did a little recollecting.

In his fifth-grade classroom he usually began the day with singing, using his guitar as instrument of choice. Music was part of the day, and often he would close the day with more singing. Even through the other details of class work and assignments, music seemed to be the interconnection.

Add to that, his whole family finds encouragement in music. His oldest son Marshall plays violin and mandolin, both of which he discovered used the same fingering. He also took up guitar using his father's guitar. Son Blake is early on to a cornet and a bass guitar. Wife Brenda was supposed to have been the one with the mandolin for her kindergarten class.

When Todd revealed this strong interest in music, I had a flashback. While at Oregon State I was taking a course that would have headed me toward civil engineering. It was linked to structural steel work. However, I was having difficulties in working out the strength and stress in mathematics. Not a good sign for one contemplating building bridges!

So I searched out the veterans' testing service. Many of us who went to college after being in WWII needed this helpful service. Service personnel, ones who especially had been in combat, had emotional wounds that needed to be healed. Often they are masked by abilities and interests.

I took a series of interest and abilities tests and discovered that the highest interest I had was music! Todd's discovery was "déjà vu all over again." But for both of us, music has been something we've used while involved in our calling. Music was not our direct calling, but a strong interest.

As I look at our family members, I see this all through them. Margaret and her VOCA camp experience uses music all the time. The songs become a part of the campers' total experience. The young campers can both recall and reinforce new ways of dealing with the abuse they've received.

Son Chris has worked in radio stations starting from being a request line answerer to being on air. His mobile DJ work parallels his work as a morning on-air DJ. He also plays lead piano for the praise band at his church.

While I was producing the Open Door radio program, music was essentially two-thirds of the program. It was "being where my listeners were living." The music is what grabbed them because it related to where they were.

Music has been an under girding for our family life. Lenore had played baritone horn, and I had played clarinet through high school. But once I left home for the Army, the instrument was left behind. I never played it again. My musical "talents" later became listening to

Bring in the Clowns—
A Metaphor for Ministry

the music for its content for Open Door, so much so that youth in the church would often ask me, "Bud, what's on top of the charts now?" and I would tell them.

This is where "Trust me" led.

Now the direct challenge is for each of us to discover not only the interest criteria, but also to see where it leads us. What creative juices do we find latent bubbling or sometimes rumbling beneath the surface?

THE CHALLENGE OF "MAKEOVER"

Few of you reading these words would take the radical route that I have in leaving one form of ministry for another. Maybe some of you will actually put on grease paint and, more importantly, learn how to become a caring clown. As I've pointed out, there are excellent resources for that route.

But what would happen if you'd do as a number of clergy I've known have done? We call it a ministerial "makeover."

Is it too difficult for you to consider exploring a field of ministry that engages even more of your talents?

Vocation has always involved risk taking. Any vocation. Think of Peter and Andrew leaving what must have been a reasonably successful fishing business to follow an itinerant preacher. They even found the business was still there three years later, only to leave it for good. Jesus said, "Follow me and leave your livelihood."

After The Gig or
Evaluating Your Ministry

The church we attend has had a number of ministerial candidates in the last few years. They considered professional ministry as at least their second career when they left for seminary.

Another friend of mine had a very high corporate office in a well-known company. But somehow, while dealing with corporate finances was fine for his bottom line, it wasn't satisfying his inner calling. He took early retirement, went to seminary, and now is a Protestant chaplain in a major hospital. Was it a scary choice, especially as an older man going back to school? You bet. But would he have done anything else? No. He even went on to get his D. Min while still doing his pastoral duties. That took John another five years!

Leaving a local church as I did is only one choice among many. Most of us still manage to be in the church setting. In that context we need to take time to check the creative abilities and interests we have.

As I've said before, putting on makeup does not make the clown. It's what is in your heart that is calling you. That's a key to local congregations. When you moved into a new place, or even in the church you are presently serving, have you made use of local statistics?

When I served as an assistant minister in Stockton, California, the senior pastor was most helpful in understanding this kind of information. He had worked in finding sites for new churches in southern California before becoming the pastor in Stockton.

Bring in the Clowns—
A Metaphor for Ministry

He was a consumer of what local governments had available for information about the communities. He would use census tracts, zone maps, and any form of information that was available including data from planning commissions. Then together with his Presbytery committee, they would determine where a new church would be considered.

Contacts within that community would then be made by people calling door-to-door to determine the interest in having a new church in the area. He used all the available information he could to make the necessary decisions.

When I left that church and came to Portland, one of the first trips I made was to the local government agencies. I found census tracts to determine the nature of the area.

Having children in a local school made it possible to obtain an awareness of what children saw as a need for themselves. When our daughter Margaret was in middle school, she felt there was a need for an after-school program for her friends. We began a once-a-week food-and-fun group that called themselves "The Mob Squad," a play on what was then the title of a popular TV program.

That later led to a rather nice high school youth group that included youth from the neighborhood. They became involved with music and had their own singing group, the Koinonia Singers. Added to their experience were a number of mission service trips, each one being nearly a month in duration. We camped out in churches, cooked our own food, did a variety of ministries including vacation Bible schools, along with working on the church buildings. Many churches now have mission trips here and abroad as a regular form of youth ministry.

Most of this came as a result of one of the key elements in ministry, listening. That's what we do in our hospital clown ministry, to be in the moment with the patients. Jesus practiced this as we read and reread his life story. Listening is central in much of the biblical accounts, specifically in dreams, visions, and other extraordinary experiences.

Have you and your congregational leadership visited the homes, apartments, and businesses—including pubs—in your area to know what is happening? Sometimes it means being willing to experience rejection as well. One elder who had been visiting within his community said, "I've had a lot of doors slammed in my face around here."

This may say something about how visitation takes place and about how we lack bonding in the communities in which we live.

As a retired clergyman, I'm often called upon to fill in when pastors are on vacation or when the pulpit is vacant. A recent experience told me a lot about one small church and its vitality. It was the Clatskanie Presbyterian Church.

Their official number of members was seventy-five, and I was asked to be there the weekend of July fourth. Their interim pastor had left and they were using a number of retirees to fill the pulpit. I rather suspected that since it was a three-day weekend, their numbers would be down. I was in for a surprise.

The bright Sunday morning found the congregation filling most of the pews. Their greetings to each other filled the air with the hearty sense of warm friendship. Lay leadership had been developed over the years by their pastors and they were ready to take charge of the service. That made my part much easier.

During one portion of the service, a gentleman stood up and asked for volunteers to help visit people in the hospital. A number stood up. Then they talked about helping out at a feeding place for homeless people in a nearby community. Volunteers again gave their names.

On top of that, they also said that on Monday, which was the Fourth of July, they would need people to get their community float ready. Two members of the church had been selected by the community to be the grand marshall and his wife in the parade.

As I later learned, the church also won the top prize for the best float in the parade. All of this was done because somewhere along the way, their pastors had

After The Gig or
Evaluating Your Ministry

empowered the members to carry on. The church was not the pastor, but the members engaged in ministry.

In our clowning we have learned to listen and let go. Lenore and I have decided to "retire" from our hospital clowning. Age is catching up with us, but we are fortunate. We have some clowns willing to give of their time to take our place. John Larsen, whom we talked about in the last chapter, has already started in the hospital.

I've felt that ministry, as I've tried to learn from my Lord, is a shared ministry. Jesus certainly showed us that with the group of people he gathered and launched.

How willing are we as pastors to let others do a ministry we think we could do better? What are our ego needs? When do we let go of them?

Clowning and its emphasis have liberated my ministry. I feel that over the more than a quarter century I've shared this ministry, I've grown greatly. In all those years I haven't developed any of the juggling, magic, or speaking skits for my clown. The intuitive and inductive side of ministry is essential, and it sometimes finds opportunity to be expressed in places we hadn't expected.

In the face-to-face encounters with others, my own life has grown even when I don't know the people involved. This was dramatically proven to both Lenore and me in a large street parade in Portland.

In early summer we have two main Portland parades. One is the annual Rose Festival parade with many fan-

Bring in the Clowns—
A Metaphor for Ministry

cifully-designed floats, bands from outside Portland, a Rose Queen and her court, plus lots of hoopla. It is a great and wonderful parade with great television and other media coverage.

A week before the Rose Parade we have "The Starlight Parade" which begins at dusk on Saturday. People dressed in all kinds of goofy costumes begin the parade with a run through town. Then come the less-than-magnificent floats, plus other bands and organizations. It is much lighter fare and a lot of fun for an early evening parade.

We have clowned in this parade a couple of times. But the first experience had unique and marvelous experiences for both Lenore and me. Rather than just walk down the middle of the street as pretty-looking clowns, we wanted to "work the crowd." That meant giving personal attention to the people crowding the sidewalks or sitting on the curbs. There are forty to fifty thousand or more people who attend these events. They are the parade lovers.

What we didn't know was that we were not supposed to "work the crowd" along the curbs. We learned that later! But that's exactly what we did. As Wrinkles, Lenore was on one side of the parade route and I as Doolotz the tramp clown was on the other side. We responded to people as they allowed us into their space. They were sitting on the curbs, in lawn chairs, or standing four and five deep on the sidewalks.

At one point, a small child took Wrinkles hand as she went along the curbs dusting off people with her feather duster. The child just stayed with her as Wrinkles moved up the block. All the time Wrinkles was expecting the child to let go and return to her parents, or the parents would be coming after the child. But it didn't happen. She came to the end of the block.

Finally Wrinkles stopped and took the child all the way back to where her family was. The child had an extraordinary experience with a clown, and Wrinkles did, too. Almost a scary moment, but yet an incredible time of absolute trust that both the child and the parent had in Wrinkles. They both found her to "be in their moment" and trustworthy. The experience embraces what we knew that caring clowning could do. It was a wonder-filled moment. It was intuitive and inductive in action.

Doolotz was the tramp clown I took on the parade. I usually don't use Zyppurr outside the hospital. As Doolotz, my job was to carry a little child's broom and dustpan down the street. I was sweeping up Portland streets one cigarette butt at a time. Using all kinds of simple antics, I would look for places along the route to deposit each stinking butt.

On occasion I could not get to a trash bin because the streets were four to six rows deep with people. With as much flair as I could manage, I would just dump that awful butt into my sport coat pocket. It later made for an awful-smelling coat and later a trip to the dry cleaners.

At one point, when I was searching for a trash barrel, a true homeless street person stepped out of the crowd. He bowed and offered his hat as a place for depositing the butt.

We made nonverbal contacts. I shook my head "no-no-no." He kept in pantomime mode and nodded "yes-yes-yes." We went back and forth for just a few moments before he came closer and put his hat right by the cigarette butt. He nodded for me to dump the cigarette butt into his hat. Reluctantly, I did. He then put on his hat.

Before I could respond to him with a hug, he slipped quickly back into the crowd and was gone. I could have floated the rest of the two-mile parade route. All the others along the route gave me a bad time when I was trying to find a place to get rid of that smelly cigarette. But one who knew rejection himself stepped forth in gentleness and offered kindness along with acceptance. It was an incredible moment for me.

I felt I had encountered the Christ in that exchange, whether the man knew that or not. Somewhere in the genes God gave him, he took the risk and stepped forth. He identified with the problem and my predicament. He came and "saved" me from my problem.

Both Lenore and I will long remember those two experiences as among the highest moments of trust and caring in our clowning. We add them to the other experiences in ministry, no matter in what avenues we found them.

A dear friend, Dr. Dick Litherland, gave us insights in another experience he helped provide for us. A small struggling interracial church in Oakland, California, had been Dick's to pastor as an interim. He invited Lenore and me to do our little clown transformation gig. Afterward, he wrote this short meditation which he sent to a group of friends.

Yesterday, vows were to be made with preparation.
Today, words are to be treated with care.
Yesterday the sermon was given silently;
without words, but carefully,

Bring in the Clowns– A Metaphor for Ministry

by two clowns acting the message
of human need and God's love.
And the people "heard" the message,
laughing, applauding, receiving, sharing.

Such care was given by the clowns
so their actions conveyed the words
without the words being spoken.
   —Ecclesiasticus 19:4-17 (focusing on vs.. 10-17
              and 2 Corinthians 5-21)

Lord, divine Word, grant me the heart to treasure your Word; the ear to treat the words I hear with respect; and the mouth to utter words with loving care. Amen.

Grace and Peace, Dick, from Oakland, California, "the other side of the Bay,"

Written Mon., Oct. 28, 1996 at 7:59 A.M.

After The Gig or
Evaluating Your Ministry

Dear Brother Dick has now moved beyond our physical presence into that realm that is offered to us all. He left a magnificent trail of writings and incredible ministries within the church and communities.

DISCOVERING YOUR GIFTS
AND THE WORLD'S NEEDS

However you look at your ministry, it is the call to be God's special person in his beloved world. You can preach it from the pulpit, and you can be the one who evidences it in your life. It helps to know how you can match your gifts with the world's need, especially those in the block where you live.

What types of gifts do you share, and how aware are you of your abilities and interests? Your calling to ministry, lay, clergy, or even clowning, always means stepping out from the crowd.

In the military I well remember how we stepped forward, usually the sergeant saying "Frimoth, take one step forward." He then would send me off to KP or some other assignment. This was not of my choice.

When we know our inclinations and evaluate their strengths, then we can take that step out of the crowd. Ministry is always about answering the call. We don't know all that happened before Jesus put his hand on Peter and Andrew to pull them out of their fishing boats. Jesus knew he could use them.

Bring in the Clowns—
A Metaphor for Ministry

He could even use that prostitute at Jacob's well on a hot day to go back into town and evangelize her neighbors. She was so moved that they believed her. Her talent was not in prostitution, but in reaching out with good news. She shared the gospel as she discovered it and found the joy of letting others know.

We often feel that the right moment needs to come before we can make a change, if change is what is working on us. A new church group in our area is being formed. No one erects a building and then seeks to add people to it. Rather, the members develop a new church by forming small groups. People get to know each other more directly and intimately as they share concerns in small groups.

Those groups then meet together for worship, but their strength begins in the small groups. Another church is working on similar groups. This time they're using materials to help build spiritual formation. It's a challenge to meet weekly for seven months sharing insights gathered from their studies and fellowship. Community is developed with all of the strengths that occur.

For a number of years many of us used these kinds of small groups for personal reflection and spiritual growth. Some included using insightful human evaluations like the Meyers/Briggs type indicators and similar tools. When we become more familiar with our own aptitudes and talents, it is up to us to discover where and how to use them.

After The Gig or
Evaluating Your Ministry

We can "step forward" knowing that as we have been called to new or renewing ministry we'll not be alone... ever! We are in God's hands, and God has chosen to use our hands.

Whose hands are these, Lord?
I look at them and wonder,
Can you really use them?
Are my hands but another metaphor
For serving you?
Is there a special rope on which
I need to pull or be pulled?
Where is the place...that important *place*
That is attracting me?
Do I dare use these hands to write a response
And then turn my deepest heartfelt feelings
Over to You...?
Oh these stirrings of the heart
That never seem to go away
To be involved more and more with Your beloved
People...
Whoever they are—maybe neighbors
Or the guy holding in his hands
His crudely printed sign at the freeway exit...
The little child who languishes in a wheelchair
And because of strange prenatal happenings
Will never speak a word or walk a step
Or be able to use her hands to draw or write....

Bring in the Clowns—
A Metaphor for Ministry

Lord, these have to be Your hands
Your healing through my calloused hands
Bringing hope and encouragement even
For just a moment...and then fading
Back into that incredible wasteland
Of an incomplete brain to comprehend
More than just this moment.

Yet these are Your hands that touched
little Charlie
And he smiled Your smile
A serendipity of grace
For an aging clown.

MOMENTS FOR REFLECTION

1. Where and how do you evaluate your ministry, your clowning experience, your involvement with your skills? What tools that are available within society, Myers/Briggs or other mental evaluative tools have you dared to take? What happened afterwards? How were you able to discern what you innately knew?

2. How do you make use of God-given gifts to move beyond a sometimes flat ministry? You can make the choice to move ahead, if that is what these tools tell you. Or if they say, "you're on track," then what? How have you taken time to discover anew your interests and gifts and then see places to implement them in ministry?

Clowning opened up areas I would never have thought I would enter. Such places as in the hospital, being invited into rooms of patients I did not know, or even into ER.

3. What gifts that you know you have are you hiding? Are you fearful that they may really be your calling, even if it means shifting out of the ministry you first felt called to follow? I never started out to be involved with radio, although as a child I had been interested a little bit. But with musical interest and some gifted youth, we were able to move well beyond anything I could ever have imagined.

   I became involved in a radio program that literally spanned the globe and brought in the writings of youth and young adults from places I'd never heard of. Have you had gifts dropped in your lap of ministry and have not known what to do with them? Believe me, when that happens, listen to that calling, and as my good wife has said on many occasions, "Go for it!" This changed my life and ministry, and with the Spirit of the living Christ calling, it can change your ministry as well.

4. The Bible says we are made in the image of God. Jesus came to give a new meaning to that image (Philippians 2:5-11). Since we are in God's image, that means we have creative abilities and

Bring in the Clowns—
A Metaphor for Ministry

talents. It may even mean your creativeness can bring new music to this generation that speaks in the language that is understood. Will it become full-time ministry for which you will need to move out of the womb of mother church and find your funding?

There are many I know who have done this in media (radio, TV, broadcasting, using all the latest multiplying electronic gadgets and tools). They are not there just for play stations and iPods. It may lead to Podcasting services. How can you use your gifts to claim them for ministry in the name of the Lord of your life?

Take that risk. Recall the words of Isaiah:

"Now thus says the Lord, He who created you,
He who formed you: Do not fear, for I have re-deemed you;
I have called you by name, you are mine.
When you pass through the waters, I will be with you;
And through the waters, they shall not overwhelm you;
When you walk thorough fire you shall not be burned,
And the flame shall not consume you.
For I am the Lord your God."
—Isaiah 43:1-3 (NRSV)

Chapter 9

Going For It–
Using Sense and Heart

Now it is your decision as to either use a few of these guidelines to model your ministry, or just stay put. Movement can be in many directions, but the choices are always with you to accept or not.

The church we attend in Portland had an annual music camp. It was a delicious experience for children from second through eighth grades. They spent every morning making sets for a musical. Practice was done with various teachers. Even dance steps were often included in the drama. All productions had biblical themes. This summer experience drew in children from the community as well as the congregation.

Children auditioned for speaking and singing parts ahead of time. The whole experience was incredible for children, leaders, and those of us who attended. In a week's time they were able to practice and produce a rather involved biblical singing drama.

Hours of preparation by staff were made well in advance. Many volunteers made the experience meaningful and the service worshipful. In addition, the children learned much more about the likes of Elijah, David, and other biblical characters. It was both fun and educational at the same time.

After each presentation, instead of a coffee hour fellowship, a luncheon was served. I was asked to have several clowns interact with the congregation as they attended this outside courtyard meal. Only one of our clowns said she would be available, but didn't want to clown alone. She was rather new to clowning, and it would have been difficult if she were the only one there.

So I said I'd be her partner. We shared several e-mails and phone calls. Although hesitant, she e-mailed me the night before to say she'd be there. I said I wanted to be "straight" during the service and play. Then I'd slip out to change into clown before the fellowship time. It meant skipping the last part of the service. That change would have to be a quick job.

We were to meet in the balcony of the church during worship. We did just that, but she said, "I'm not going to clown. I'm just going to be part of the congregation."

It threw me because she was a good clown with excellent talent. Here was an opportunity for her to "go for it," to practice her skills. I was to be there to support her, but now I was to be the only clown. But it was her choice and I accepted her reason.

With my years of experience, I managed through the hour and found enjoyment with the experience. Most of it was done non-verbally. My clown friend also attended the luncheon and visited with congregational members. No one but Lenore and I knew her decision.

This caused me to wonder about you, the reader of these lines. Do you just fantasize what you want to accomplish, or is there a bit of daring in you to "risk" the opportunities that come your way?

For a year or two when we first moved into our present home I wondered how best to get to know our neighbors. Then one of them put on a block party! It was an enjoyable, non-threatening way to share a pot-luck meal and discover that there are people who are interested in knowing one another.

Since that time, it has been my pleasure to work with the block party for several years. A neighbor has a tiny but lovely park-like area that we used for three hours. A large apple tree provided refreshing shade from the late-afternoon sun. People came and left as they desired. Delicious foods of all sorts were shared, as well as great conversations.

One year a member of the committee thought it would be great for people to tell the history they knew of their homes. One man who still lived in the area was the contractor for many of the homes. He brought a folder of advertisements he published when he began building in the area. People pored over these yellowed newspaper ads and marveled at some of the photos taken of the area forty years before when some of the roads were just dirt.

In order to help get to know each other, on the nametags people wore was a line telling how many years they had lived in the area. Recent people marveled at the stories about the area from those who had lived here for many years.

But perhaps the most important experiences of all were the personal conversations. Many of them included words like, "When you're out walking in the neighborhood, knock on our door. If we're home, stop in for a cup of coffee or tea. That way we can get to know each other better."

The point of this example is quite obvious. We have to extend ourselves to reach out to others. A wave of the hand to a passing neighbor is one thing. To invite people into your home is to open your life to others. Our homes reflect who we are.

In ministry, openness to others is the first step as a clown using the "risk encouragement." Waiting for others to come to you is often wishful thinking. Remember the beautifully-costumed clown Lenore experienced early in her clowning? He just stood there for people to observe, not moving to be involved. Some people extend themselves more easily than others because they have the outgoing natural abilities and instincts.

For those more introverted or shy, the risk to step out from fear of rejection is a major move. Interestingly, many clergy are more comfortable in the pulpit than in the homes of their parishioners. Again, remember who is on stage and who is the audience. You need to know your congregation in their home setting in order to be able to meet them and their needs in the church setting. Sometimes it happens during crises in the home and you learn more about the family.

When you consider yourself to be "on stage," then all of the emphasis is on you. You have to be perfect or close to it whether in preaching, clowning, or visiting in a home.

But those same experiences of reaching out can be learned and honed. Clowning has taught me to move into spaces I never expected to enter. Many were beyond my comfort zone. But now I find it easier to reach out.

Ministry as a profession has likewise led me to very sacred places in the lives of people. One of the very poignant experiences is to sit with a dying patient, holding hands beside the bed. Once it led to an interesting opportunity

In my first parish I had to call elder Cecil Herron out of his farming field. The reason? An older woman who was dying had never been baptized and wanted to make her confession of faith. We didn't have time to call a Session meeting or examine the woman's faith.

Cecil had been on his tractor when I called.

Going For It—Using Sense and Heart

His wife Hazel went out into the field to tell him the need. He quickly washed up and drove into town to serve as the elder for baptism. We decided that we'd inform the Session after the fact of baptism.

Can you see that Cecil and I were the "audience" and Marie was "on stage"? Going through the more formal way of a Session meeting and questioning the reason the woman wanting the sacrament wouldn't have worked. There wasn't time.

Those understanding Session elders later didn't raise any questions about our actions. They made the baptism a part of Session records, and we offered a prayer of gratitude for the opportunity to serve in Christ's name.

Serendipities are offered many days in ministry, but we hesitate to allow them an opportunity. My clown friend who backed out of the experience missed the joy in the faces of the congregation as the clown moved about. I'm not sure she regretted not clowning, nor did I question her about her decision.

However, I did send her an e-mail to let her know I was disappointed that she missed the opportunity to share her gifts. I let her know I honored her decision not to clown, but felt she let an opportunity slip by her. It might make the next one even more difficult to accept. She remains a friend and often sends thoughtful information to me via email.

"Going for it" almost always means being a bit out of step with the rest of the world. Someone said that

Bring in the Clowns—
A Metaphor for Ministry

Thomas Edison had a thousand failures before he made the first light bulb work, but he kept experimenting.

From more than fifty years of ministry, with half including clowning, I have found more doors opened when I "went for it." With the radio ministry, I asked listeners to share their prose. It would have been much easier to have written my own stuff, because I knew the direction I wanted to go with an idea. But to entertain the thought that others might have better ways of expressing that idea required an openness that often was not easy, but oh, how rewarding.

One afternoon when I was in the study at the church I received a phone call from 62KGW radio. It was from the Public Affairs director of the station.

Joan asked, "Bud, are you sitting down?"

"Of course, I'm at my desk working on a sermon for Sunday. Why do you ask?"

"Well, Open Door has just won a George Foster Peabody Award."

"So?" I asked.

"Bud, this is the highest award in broadcasting! People like Alistair Cooke, Mr. Kangaroo (Bob Keeshan), the 'Today' morning TV program are among the other winners."

"That's pretty good company, but what else does it mean?"

"KGW is sending you and the station manager, Dean Woodring, to New York City to receive the award. Do you think you can get the time off?"

Going For It—Using Sense and Heart

The Session did allow me that opportunity, and what a gift that surprise became. I knew I wasn't the one who had done all of the work on the program that had been submitted. In fact, Gloria Chandler was the person who strongly suggested that we send in a tape of the program called "Insanity." She was the personal secretary to Mrs. Bullit, the owner of King Broadcasting of which 62 KGW was a part.

This was a most promising serendipity, because the program that won the award had been mostly written by our sixteen-year-old-daughter, Margaret, and Steve Johnson, another teen. I had helped smooth out some of the timing questions and a few other details with which I was comfortable.

But to have won this prestigious award was unheard of. We had been producing the program for less than two years. The Open Door readers were all teenage students. My part was simply to help put the thirty-minute program together and time it. Our recording engineer, Gordon Miller, was also a top man in his field and for 62KGW. His advice during the production of the program was invaluable.

That was the first of more than forty national and international awards the program received during its twenty-one years of broadcasting. It literally opened new doors of possibilities I had never imagined. In seminary we had a course in radio. At the time, I never dreamed radio would become such an important ingredient for nearly half my professional ministry.

Taking the risk to try something that had only been a kind of wild interest proved to become a ministry in itself. It kept my interest for more than twenty years and later provided a profession for our son Chris.

"Going for it" happens in local churches, too.

Eleanor D. never thought she could lead a service of worship when I was absent from the church one Sunday, but I had asked her. She was an Elder and I felt she could do it. Finally, she said OK. She thought she'd just read a sermon from one of my many books of sermons. I encouraged this rather prim and proper schoolteacher to write her own sermon. With reasoned thought, she put together an excellent sermon.

She was stunned by the response of the congregation. They often quoted her words to her for several years afterwards. This is interesting to me, because I'm not sure how many did that with my words!

Risking, going for it, or whatever phrase you want to use means that you have to trust. Sometimes people let you down when they promise to be supportive. All of us know that experience when friends turn out not to be the friends we anticipated.

In ministry, trusting the Spirit to guide you is crucial. But that Spirit also says be as prepared as you can before you make that decision. When I split from pastoring a church and doing Open Door, there was more trust than preparation. However, the church allowed me three months to get my act together before leaving. It allowed Lenore to find her part-time job and me to work out some details with the Open Door board.

There is no doubt in my mind that God's presence was in this direction. I believed his words "Trust me" still ring true twenty-five year later.

Can I guarantee that in six weeks after reading this book you'll know a difference in your ministry or clowning? And what would those steps be?

Certainly these are often calculated moves. As a Presbyterian clergyman, I had our denomination's clergy placement system to consider. I used it when I first left seminary. But more than that, I had friends who knew when I was ready to make a move. They forwarded my name to pastor-seeking committees who followed up in their contacting. It's a fairly normal and helpful way to find a new challenge.

In veering from that normal track by leaving the pastoral ministry, I discovered new ways of ministry. While I can't play any musical instrument, when asked, I'd tell people I "played a mean CD." Yet I had an even greater appreciation for music I heard. I could put it into a context with which the listeners could connect. Their "stages," which really were their writings, became the fertile ground into which their ideas were sown.

Bring in the Clowns—
A Metaphor for Ministry

In clowning I moved from being "on stage" to "listening to others" whom I was called to serve. A pre-schooler screamed and ran the other way when she first saw me in my clown outfit. As she clung to her mother's skirt, she turned and yelled, "Leave me alone!" I happened to come upon her by chance, but she didn't know that. Her "stage" told me what her "audience" needed to do. So I moved in the other direction.

I learned of another way to help those frightened of clowns, but I had some help. It was the annual Festival of Trees celebration that is sponsored by the Providence Portland Child Center for Medically Fragile Children. A huge convention hall was rented. Incredibly beautiful displays of Christmas trees with decorations filled the room. Local school children and youth provided vocal and instrumental music on stage. All the while, people of all ages wandered from display to display.

One time as I was clowning non-verbally among the crowds of people, I kept catching the eye of a middle school girl. She'd make a quick glance and then rush away with her friends. I didn't think a lot about it even after having the experience with her a number of times as I worked with the crowd of people.

A little later, three or four of this girl's friends brought her to me. They said that the girl was afraid of clowns and thought that I was trying to bother her. It caught me by surprise, so I broke my silence.

I asked the friends to ask her what did I do that frightened her. "Oh nothing. It's just your being a clown."

They also asked why I didn't talk when I clowned. I thought it would be a good way to help the young girl know that I wasn't there to scare anyone. I said that I didn't talk because they were more important than anything I could say, clever or not. I did not want to move into their space unless invited. My words wouldn't matter to them. I felt that she and her friends became more important than I was. That, to me, is what a caring clown decides. Simple actions often say more than words.

I'll never know if this helped the middle school girl, but I do know that she smiled at me and said, "Thank you." That's enough.

In ministry of any kind, I've been foisting upon you this idea of being the audience, not being on stage, even if it appears that you are on stage. Pulpits are notorious for giving that appearance of being "on stage." After all, most pulpits are raised up mainly to enable the parishioners to see who is talking. Raised pulpits are not intended to elevate the clergy. That is a hard fact clergy must face. Being "lifted up" literally can be very ego satisfying. But that is not what ministry is about.

No matter how you minister, if you learn the difference between being on stage or being audience, that ministry will slowly and even perceptibly change. It changed my thinking and expressions in the pulpit. Being a pastor can be very heady stuff and very dangerous, too. You begin to act like you are on stage while forgetting the audience.

But those on that stage can learn that they have a responsibility as well. You, being their audience, need to have them speak loudly enough for you to hear. They can let you know what their needs and concerns are.

Your words to them, when not clowning, are to ask for clarification. That can mean really becoming their audience. Active listening is often difficult, because you can almost anticipate what those on stage are going to say.

Then the serendipities come in. Those are the unexpected experiences. In our hospital clowning, the woman who said with utter simplicity after our time with her, "I'm ready to go to hospice now," gave us chills of the Spirit. Quite unexpectedly, we had become a channel for her to accept what lay ahead.

In pastoral ministry by lay and clergy, we all have wondrous tales to share, but most of the time we honor those who shared them and keep them to ourselves. We offer a prayer of gratitude for being able to be about ministry in any dimension.

If anyone tells you ministry in any form is an easy profession, don't believe it. Jesus called the twelve, knowing that one of them was going to betray him. Yet, he called Judas Iscariot to be part of the dozen he chose.

Going For It—Using Sense and Heart

If you are a pastor, how would you like those twelve on your Session or church board? Yet Jesus chose twelve different men with differing talents.

That's a component that risk ministry brings. There have been and will be experiences that are damning to you and with those among whom you minister. But there will be many that uplift and lead you into new ways of living. The other eleven disciples certainly lived different lives. Those disciples are the reason you and I are even writing and reading about ministry.

"Going for it" is hard work and so deeply experiential that it is often difficult to decipher. Perspective is hard to imagine when you take that first step out of the boat as Peter did, thinking he could also walk on water. Jesus continued to encourage him, even with other failures Peter exhibited. That kind of encouragement is still present as the Spirit leads us.

WHERE "GOING FOR IT" CAN LEAD

What have I learned from these different-but-similar forms of ministry that have called me that I can distill into a few words?

1. Discover God's words for you. Years ago I read books by Fr. Michael Quoist, a priest who wrote fantastic prayers that I often used in services of worship. In one of his books he wrote that God

gives everyone special words. These are words to live by.

On several occasions when I was a Sunday pulpit supply, I would ask people if they had special words they felt came from God just for them. Some responded in the service of worship. Others talked about them during the coffee hour.

Many people said they had been afraid to say anything about them because they weren't sure what others might say. It does sound odd, but I think my much more evangelical friends would laugh at us. They hear these words all the time and accept them.

You will know when those words are yours. They will stick with you and come to you in all kinds of settings. Trust them. See them in the context of the life of Jesus. See them in the context of your life. You are not weird. You have been blessed. Ask close friends if they know their words. Perhaps the good Lord is saying, "I'm your audience and here is what you seem to be saying you need."

2. Dare to risk. We are so afraid to lose what we have worked hard to gain. This has little to do with finances, houses, cars, or any other thing. To move on an inner calling is the willingness to trust the one who called you and gave you your words.

Going For It—Using Sense and Heart

You may wish there was an easier way to go. I just don't know any other way. When the opportunity comes your way, if you don't give it good thought and prayer, it will be passed to someone else. If your word from your Maker calls you to extend yourself, dare to extend yourself. There are awesome experiences that occur.

When we now visit our son Todd in whatever country in which he is teaching, bringing the clowns along is part of the trip. If we had not taken the risk to become clowns, the incredible experiences on four continents would never have happened. It all began for me on the hard floor of a motel in Florida asking Floyd Shaffer, "What am I doing here?"

3. Trust your process that means trust your literally God-given gifts of who you are. I didn't know I had any talent in producing a thirty-minute radio show. It had never occurred to me until it was laid in my lap. I could have rejected that call, as did a couple of pastors with whom I worked at first. They went on to other ministries that had called them. I was left to develop Open Door.

Part of that process was to be a good listener, the audience idea I've been stressing. One of my first radio/studio engineers, Richard Miller, although thirty years younger than I am, knew a great deal more about radio than I did.

Bring in the Clowns—
A Metaphor for Ministry

He said words to me that rattle my brain cage to this day, "Bud, if you're going to do this program, spend the time to do it right. No short cuts. Take the time to do it right."

Within the first year or so of producing Open Door, I would write one program and two teens would put together a couple more. One Tuesday evening, Margaret and Steve said they were too busy, "Why don't we just repeat one of our programs from a year ago? That would be a neat way out of a dilemma.

Somehow, that didn't quite fit my idea of commitment. Although I had pastoral duties to perform during the day, I spent a great deal of that night putting together a new program using ideas from our listeners.

Over the years, Margaret has often reminded herself and others that "Dad just wouldn't let us chicken out of our responsibility. It was too important. We learned then to carry out what we promised we would do. It still holds true today. "

Richard's youthful but mature wisdom has carried through into many phases of my ministry—pastoral, clowning, or being the chair of a small block party committee. Do it right even if it takes longer, which it usually does. That's trusting the process because in that process runs the Spirit of the living God.

That same process continued with my last recording engineer, Robert Strong. He learned editing and recording with Richard's help. Consequently, he helped produce a couple dozen of the programs for which Open Door received national or international awards.

The wonderful dedication of the youth and young adults over the twenty-one years also reflected their willingness to make a difference. Often they would stand in the rain or snow waiting to catch a bus to the radio station. They didn't want to fail to respond. Open Door was their program and they knew other youth and young adults around the world would be waiting to hear the program and possibly discover one of their writings being read. How great was their gift to their unseen others through the medium of radio.

4. Most importantly, give thanks. Give thanks for the calling to ministry in whatever capacity it may be. It doesn't matter if you are clergy or layperson. Give thanks, even when you are up

Bring in the Clowns–
A Metaphor for Ministry

to your eyeballs in paper or concerns. Even when the hours are so long that you are wearied to the bone, give thanks for this gift of ministry.

Going For It—Using Sense and Heart

I haven't heard too many clergy who are bitter about their calling. They may reflect on the difficulties they have to endure, but they stay with it. Lay people often have the same experiences with the clergy.

Yet, give thanks. Remember time and again the tough route that Jesus and the early disciples took. Trace the history of the church through the ages. Look at some of the mission folk in places in the world where their lives are threatened because they are helping the poor and displaced of the country.

Ministry in any form isn't meant to be on easy street. It's more like that old phrase attributed to Notre Dame football coach Knute Rockne, "When the going gets tough, the tough get going." True toughness has a tenderness to it that sees the work ahead as an opportunity of grace and gratitude.

Pastor Jim Moiso says time and time again, "Mercy. I can't believe I've been called to do this. I'm so very grateful."

Gratitude underscores all ministry. With it, unconditional love continues to flow. Trust is discovered. Risks are taken. God's words for you are heard. The process of ministry moves on in grace-filled acceptance.

Lord of all life,
How incredibly gracious
Becomes your calling.
How often I would like to forget it.

Bring in the Clowns–
A Metaphor for Ministry

I feel so inadequate, so unprepared.
Forgive my procrastinations,
My flimsy excuses,
My inner desire to be "on stage"
So people would adore me.
How can I say that
When I recall those few
Who dared remain
At the foot of your cruel cross,
You who appeared to be "on stage"
Were really an audience.
For you told John
To care for your mother,
And in the garden on Easter day
You were audience again.
When you caught Mary's anxiety
By simply calling out her name,
Her identity,
Giving her that hope
Which spirals up to this day,
And these words
That flow from where I do not know.
But I thank you
With tears of gratitude
That splash upon the keys
Of this electronic contraption.
Thank you...thank you...thank you.
Amen and Amen!

Addendum

Clowning, as usually conceived, is considered enter-tainment, and rightly so. But if you have caught the definite twist in this book, you may have discovered a different dimension. Entertaining is a wonderful way of lifting the spirits of people. Laughter gives a sense of hope; and oh, how we need it in our strife-ridden world today. This is because laughter provides perspective, and with it comes a sense of hope.

There is another dimension that is hinted at during the writing. Clowning, like other forms of ministry, deals with justice and working toward making a wrong into a right. There are times when we can't be sure that it occurs, but we are part of a process. That begins again with knowing who the audience is.

Bring in the Clowns–
A Metaphor for Ministry

One February Friday night, Lenore and I popped into a feeding program for homeless and low-income people. The program was a combined effort of many churches in northeast Portland. We gave as many people attention as possible. Wrinkles dusted off people with a gentle touch. I was handing out our little "free hug" certificates.

One homeless person looked at me and essentially asked, "Do you really mean it? The hugging?"

As Zyppurr, I nodded. This man was clothed in dark and dirty clothes. He obviously hadn't shaved for days. But he stood and we hugged. His breath had a tinge of alcohol on it.

"I'm so tired," he said as he very strongly hugged me, "I'm cold and my feet hurt."

He paused for a moment while we embraced. Others at the tables continued to eat. They weren't listening to this man and me. They had their own concerns. Then, with tears in his voice, the man struggled to ask me a penetrating question.

"Tell me, Jesus, is there any hope for me?"

All that this old clown could do was to continue to hug him.

It was true that the social agencies might be able to provide him with more comfortable shoes. This cooperative church feeding program could offer him not only food, but the warmth he needed from the cold Oregon weather for a part of an evening. But the answer of hope was more penetrating. Perhaps the most I could do was to make that hug mean that he was still a man loved, not just by an old clown, but by a loving God.

How people fall into homelessness or wander into poor housing has multiple reasons. One hug on a winter's night couldn't have solved the problem. I have no way of knowing what became of him. I'm not sure I would have known the man again on another Friday night. All I provided for him was an honest closeness he may not have felt from anyone for a long, long time.

Is that a justice issue? It certainly has that kind of feeling. We could analyze why he had fallen from hope and offer all kinds of counseling, but could we have brought him back? I have a little void when I think of him from time to time. For a moment, Zyppurr offered him a loving hug. Each of us is one of God's beloved children.

Had I met a disguised Jesus? "Inasmuch as you have done it to one of the least of these, you have done it to me. " And if so, what more could or should I have done?

Clowning and ministry are alike in that we end up with many more questions than answers. What makes a desperately ill patient smile when she coyly and somewhat grumpily questions clowns entering her room,

"Well, what are you doing here?"

I suspect what we were attempting to do was respond to her "stage presence" as her audience. We let her take the first step by asking the question or even her allowing us to enter the private domain of her hospital room. That was one bit of "power" she still could act upon. She exercised that power by inviting us in.

Wrinkles and Zyppurr are merely tools in ministry, our attempt is to be loving and caring. That's what Bishop K.H. Ting of the Chinese Christian Church said justice is.

"If love spreads throughout humankind, it becomes justice," (*Love Never Ends,* p. 268). To which the words of Paul Tillich might be added: "Love makes justice just."

Self-forgetting love is unconditional love shared as intense but often smiling concern and compassion. Clowns have discovered that justice becomes a freeing experience.

Makeup and costumes don't make the clown. Instead, they help to dramatize the joy that's possible even in the worst of times. I've read of some funeral homes that have caring clowns on their staff. Hospice clowns are found in many places.

Some of the most troubling medical problems children and adults experience can find a moment of encouragement from a clown's appearance. We have experienced it in ER settings where the patient speaks another language. But somehow the language of no words but caring actions covers the distance to the heart and head.

Addendum

The appreciative smile on the patient's face, or the tiny tear in the eye of a mother with a very ill child in her arms needs no words. That crooked smile that is torn between a cry and a smile lets the old clowns know that love has been shared. The mother allowed us into the ER room for just a moment. She opened her heart because she thought her child would find a tiny light of joy in the midst of frightening illness.

Is that justice? Is that compassion? Is that intrusion? We do not force our way into their presence. The important persons are not the clowns, but those who have allowed Wrinkles and Zyppurr to come into their space.

Even if it is only for a moment.

And don't forget those ER staff people. When we offered them the "Rx for smiles," they often said, "I really need this today!" And then they'd almost double over with laughter at the one-liner. That was their thanks!

Tell me, is that justice? Justice somehow has to be measured with compassion or it's merely a legal transaction. Unconditional love does not measure whether or not there will be a favorable response.

Sometimes, clowns and clergy have been told where to go! Love can be spurned. Jesus knew it, and the cross reflects that rejection. So we shouldn't be surprised when our caring response is spurned. The meaning is clear. Rejecting persons are on the stage and are in control. But that doesn't stop us from offering love. We plant it like a seed in the soil of their souls. We bid that God's Spirit provides the growth.

Perhaps that's the meaning of "letting go" once we have "gone for it"! Compassion is slippery when we try to hold on to that moment. Clowning has taught us that message time and time again.

We seldom see the same persons again in the hospital. If we do, they have to tell us. We see our place as first steps in the loving process. The nurses, doctors, aides, and even those cleaning the halls and rooms do the continued caring. But even their efforts come to a close when patients are released.

Ministry has with it that heart-rending experience of letting persons go and not ever knowing what happened to them. I learned this while doing the radio program over the twenty-one years. I met very few of the listeners in person. However, a couple have kept in touch with me and continue to share their life's experiences. They're no longer teen teenagers, but well into middle adulthood.

But there are exceptions. Ministry in local churches allows for a more ongoing connection when possible. But even there people move, get married, have illnesses and the certainty of deaths. When you know you are the audience, you can let them go off to new stages. Letting go once you have "gone for it" is one of the hardest of experiences in ministry. However, it can be one of the loveliest when it brings us around again to the word justice.

When you let go, you give wings to another person. Every thoughtful teacher, clergy person, doctor, parent, or friend knows how hard that can be. Yet the experience of seeing another person fly solo and knowing that you had a part in their learning is what ministry can provide. You as the audience can applaud the one you encouraged to "go for it" and seize the day.

> She still writes to me
> Of her deepest concerns,
> Much like she had done
> Years before when we
> Used her thoughtful prose
> In a youth and young adult
> Radio program.
> Life has changed a great deal
> For her as she reaches out
> To find her place in God's sun.
> As a maturing single adult
> Her experiences are far different
> From ones with which I'm familiar.
> She has abilities to fathom
> Some of the depths of other
> People's needs with insights
> That sometimes frighten her.
> She has shared some with me
> That I certainly cannot explain

Bring in the Clowns–
A Metaphor for Ministry

And which she feels are deeply
Related with Jesus who is her friend.
She somehow wants me to bless
Her awe-filled experience,
And this raises all kinds
Of old theological hackles.
But somehow what she says
Finds a degree of reliability
That astounds me and
Also frightens me
Because she has tapped
Into the very heart of love
And its beat both thrills
As well as alarms her.
Am I right to support
This seemingly quasi-religious
Experience in order
To offer spiritual protection
Or let her just dangle
And discover the awesome
Dimensions into which
She now has moved....?
Which is more important,
Spiritual rightness
Or supportive compassion?
It seems justice
Is never quite simple.

Appendix – Theories of Intelligence

Following are the web sites for theories of intelligence that Todd Frimoth has used:

http://www.lth3.k12.il.us/rhampton/mi/mi.html

http://www.thirteen.org/edonline/concept2class/mi/index.html

http://www.thomasarmstrong.com/multiple_intelligences.htm

http://www.newcityschool.org/innovations/mi/home.html

http://www.ldpride.net/learningstyles.MI.htm#Multiple%20Intelligences%20Explained

Bring in the Clowns—
A Metaphor for Ministry

INVENTORIES AND SURVEY/TESTS FOR INTELLIGENCES

http://www.ldrc.ca/projects/miinventory/mitest. html

http://surfaquarium.com/MI/inventory.htm

http://jeffcoweb.jeffco.k12.co.us/high/wotc/confli3. htm

Joy for Free!

Worship on the Lord's Day at Kenilworth Presbyterian Church

Feb. 8, 1970 4 o'clock

"Where you have known joy, you have known
Him"

BANNER AND POSTER ENTER

"C'mon And Get Happy!"   Jazz Combo

Statement of welcome

Bring in the Clowns—
A Metaphor for Ministry

THE JOY OF EXPECTANCY

"On the Street Where You Live"   Jazz Combo
"On a Clear Day"   The Sophisticates
    Reading: "Take a world"
"What's New?"   Jazz Combo

THE JOY OF PLANNING

    Reading: "Reach out in the darkness"
"Take the 'A' Train"   Jazz Combo
    Reading: "Man-making"
"Stairways to the Stars"   Jazz Combo

THE JOY OF HUMAN LOVE

    Reading: "Shall I compare thee to a summer's day?"
"Lover"   Jazz Combo
    Reading: Are You Running With Me, Jesus?"
        A prayer of Malcom Boyd
"A Man and a Woman"   The Sophisticates
    Reading: "Comparisons"
"You're Nobody 'Til Somebody   Jazz Combo
    Loves You"

THE JOY OF NATURAL BEAUTY

    Reading: "Life's common things"
"Mountain Greenery"   Jazz Combo

Joy for Free!

"The Song of the Jet"   The Sophisticates
    Reading: Psalm 104:1-4
"Blue Skies"   Jazz Combo

A time for mingling and greeting one another

THE JOY OF FREEDOM

"The Sunny Side of the Street"   Jazz Combo
    Reading: "Born Free"
"Do You Know the Way   The Sophisticates
    to San Jose?"
      Reading: "Prayer in the secular city"
"I've Got the World on a String"   Jazz Comb

THE JOY OF ACCEPTANCE

    Reading: "Old friendship"
"Back in Your Own Backyard"   Jazz Combo
"This Is All I Ask"   The Sophisticates
    Reading: "Paul Tillich on acceptance"
"It's Wonderful"   Jazz Combo
    Reading: "New songs"

Benediction
"He's Got the Whole World   Everyone sings!
    in His Hands"

Bring in the Clowns–
A Metaphor for Ministry

The Jazz Combo was made up of the following instruments: piano, guitar, drums, upright bass, sax, trumpet, and trombone.

The Sophisticates were a group of five young adult women with a pianist.

Readers were youth, young adults, mid adults, and senior adults.

The M.A.W.D. committee was composed of youth and adults. M.A.W.D means Music, Art, Worship, Drama.

SOURCES OF INSPIRATION FOR THE DAY:

"I repeat: God is not against us, He is for us...God is no killjoy!" Karl Barth

"Joy is the experience Jesus points to as the outermost limit and goal of all that He came in God's name and with God's power to give." Frederick Buechner

"I have told you this so that my joy may be in you and that your joy may be complete." Jesus Christ

Pantomime Psalm 139

(This is a psalm to pantomime. Lenore took each phrase and offered actions. Many psalms are excellent possibilities. The reason for the pantomime is to provide a visual reminder of the words. One can also receive this when you watch a sign language interpreter. Their words are most visual to the person for whom sound is gone.)

Lord, you examine me and know me,
> (hands upraised, then down together at the chest)

You know if I am standing or sitting,
> (hands up for standing, then down for sitting)

You read my thoughts from far away,
> (hands to the head, then reach far away)

Bring in the Clowns—
A Metaphor for Ministry

Whether I walk
   (she takes a few steps)
Or lie down,
   (she puts hands together and lays head on
   them)
You are watching,
   (she puts hands cupped as if looking down)
You know every detail of my conduct.
   (with finger wagging she acts like counting)
The word is not even on my tongue, Lord, before
   you know all about it;
   (hand to the mouth and then lifted up along
   with raised eyes)
You fence me around, both behind me and in front
   of me, shielding me with your hand.
   (makes motion of surrounding herself and then
   throwing her hands upwards as a shield)
Such knowledge is beyond my understanding, a
   height to which my mind cannot attain.
   (points to her head, then reaches as high as possible while gently shaking her head)
Where could I go to escape your spirit? Where could
   I flee from your presence?
   (hands on each side of the face, cupping the face
   if looking for a place to flee)
If I climb to the heavens, you are there,
   (upward sweep of hands high)
There, too, if I lie in the depths of despair.
   (hands clasped at breast and head bowed deeply
   in sorrow)

Pantomime Psalm 139

If I flew to the point of the sunrise,
    (hands quickly sweep toward the east)
Or westward across the sea,
    (hands and body sweep toward the west)
Your hand would still be guiding me, your right
    hand holding me.
    (hands raised and clasped as if being held
    above)
If I asked the darkness to cover me and the light to
    become night around me,
    (hands over head as if darkness and head
    bowed)
That darkness would not be dark to you, night would
    be as light as day.
    (hands open up and arms raised up high)
It was you who created my inmost self and put me
    together in my mother's womb;
    (hands together across the lower abdomen)
For all these mysteries I thank you:
    (right hand upwards left hand at side)
For the wonder of myself,
    (both hands clasped at the breast)
For the wonder of your works.
    (head upwards and hands sweeping to right and
    left)
You know me through and through from having
    watched my bones take shape when I was formed
    in secret, knitted together in the limbo of the
    womb.

Bring in the Clowns—
A Metaphor for Ministry

    (left hand on chest, right hand twisting as if
    shaping a fetus)

You scrutinized my every action, all were recorded
    in your book,

    (left hand like a book, right hand as if writing a
    list)

My days listed and determined even before the first
    of them occurred.

    (holding up hand as if with a book and with
    other hand checking off items)

God, how hard it is to grasp your thoughts! How
    impossible to count them!

    (hands on either side of head, rocking it back
    and forth but eyes looking upward in awe)

I could no more count them, than I could count
    the sand,

    (one hand over the other acting as if letting sand
    go from one hand to the other)

And even if I could, you would still be with me.

    (shaking her head in disbelief, then looking joy-
    fully upwards)

God, examine me and know my heart,

    (right hand raised up for examination and then
    to the heart)

Probe me and know my thoughts,

    (fingers to both sides of the head like a probe)

Make sure I do not follow hurtful ways

    (an "oh no" shaking of the head)

Then guide me in the way that is everlasting.

Pantomime Psalm 139

(right hand raised upward as she leaves the sanctuary)

(The Amen is spoken)

—Scripture from
the Jerusalem Bible translation.

Order of Worship

Taizé Healing and Wholeness Service
Westminster Presbyterian Church Portland, Oregon

Third Saturday of the month 5:30 to 6:30 P.M.

Prelude

Welcome by Pastor or Lay Leader

Opening Scripture

Songs for Gathering

(from "Songs and prayers from Taizé")

"It is good to trust" #11

"When the night becomes dark" #25

"Spirit of Christ Jesus" #34

Scripture reading Acts 3:1-10 (read by woman lay reader)

Bring in the Clowns—
A Metaphor for Ministry

Moments for Silent Reflection (usually five minutes)

Prayers of Intercession
(Pastor or lay leader offers a series of brief prayers, original or from prayer sources. Each is followed by the singing of a single verse from a Taizé song. After the third prayer and response, the music stops. There is an insert in the bulletin that contains the names of individuals, groups, nations, concerns that are read as a prayer by all who are in attendance. The music is then played as instrumental under a fourth and last prayer by the leader after which the song is sung one more time.)

LAYING ON OF HANDS/
LIGHTING CANDLES OF PRAYER

(During this time of singing, congregants are encouraged to come forward to receive anointing and laying on of hands. It is also a time to come forward to light a candle or candles symbolic of prayers that are being offered. It is a very reflective time of quiet music, sung, hummed, or just listened to.)

We adore You, Christ Jesus #39
My soul is at rest # 38
Veni Sancte Spiritus #41

Order of Worship

(These are sung while people are coming forward to one of the three kneelers where two prayer-team members offer listening to their requests or their silence; with their permission a small bit of oil is used for anointing their foreheads in the sign of the cross, hands are laid upon the head and shoulders, a prayer by a team member is offered, then we remain silent in the presence of God, after which the second team member closes with prayer. Those coming forward determine when they will leave the kneeler.)

(After the last person who has come forward has left, the prayer team members kneel for their own prayers, then surround the tables on which the candles have been lit. They light their own candles and join hands around the table. The leader offers a brief prayer of gratitude and assurance. The prayer team returns to the front pew, and the last song is sung.)

Song of Gratitude
"Send Your Spirit to dwell in our hearts"
      (sung three times)

Closing sentence by the leader
People leave as they are ready. No music is played.
      (This is a sample from June, 2005)

Simple Pantomime with Explanation

The first Sunday after Christmas or Epiphany Sunday is often a time when retired pastors receive calls to lead worship. The regular pastor has a desire for one Sunday off after the busy Advent and Christmas season. Along the way I came across a poignant Russian folk tale that also had a song that could be sung later on. It is called "Baboushka." It deals with searching for the elusive star over Bethlehem. There is a "Baboushka's Carol" that could be sung after the story is told. With or without the music, the idea of a simple pantomime is there.

Here is the transcript I used with several congregations.

Bring in the Clowns—
A Metaphor for Ministry

BABOUSHKA

Setting: Think of an older woman, dressed some-what in old Russian style with a basket and a few tools that you'll learn about as the story unfolds. It is from a lovely book. Later you could add "Baboushka's Carol" which a guitarist and soloist could sing. The music is in the book.

There's an old Russian folk tale that might help us understand the time immediately after Christmas. It's the story of Baboushka, a peasant woman. Lenore will pantomime the story as I tell it. Baboushka was a hard-working woman. She kept her house very clean. Her only child had died when he was quite young, so the toys she had for him were now in a basket that had become dusty with age.

One cold evening, the snow was swirling around her small house. She sat cozily by the fire drinking tea. Then there was a knock on her door. Baboushka opened her door and saw three richly-dressed men. They carried boxes of jewels, sweet oils, and ointment.

They said, "Come with us, Baboushka. We're fol-lowing a brilliant star. A young baby is born where this star shines down. He is said to be the one who will rule the world."

Baboushka replied, "The night is cold and I have so much work to do to keep my house clean. I can't come with you now."

Simple Pantomime with Explanation

After feeding the three men, she sent them on their way because they wanted to leave while it was night. That way they could follow the brilliant star. With them gone, Baboushka returned to cleaning her house. Eventually, because she became tired, she stopped for tea.

As she rocked by the fire, she thought of how she loved babies. So she decided to set out to follow the star. But before she could go, she had to clean off the dusty toys she had made for her only son who had died. She worked late into the night and was so tired she had to sit down and rest. In a short time, she fell asleep.

When she awoke it was daylight and the star was not shining. So she wrapped herself in her large shawls to keep warm. She gathered herself together and left her little house. Baboushka started on her trip, carrying small gifts in her basket.

(During this time Lenore goes down the aisle pantomiming the question and people just shake their heads to her.)

When she met someone she would ask, "Where is the baby Prince? I have some toys for him."

They would answer, "Far away from here."

So on and on she went, knocking at the doors of houses as she passed, asking everyone, "Is the baby here?"

She even came to where the baby Jesus had been born, but the family had already left. As the tradition goes, Baboushka is still looking for the Christ child.

Bring in the Clowns—
A Metaphor for Ministry

Time means nothing in the search for things that are real. Year after year she goes from house to house knocking and asking, "Is he here? Is the Christ child here?"

If she hears about a child who has been doing good deeds, she will reach into her basket and leave a gift, just in case that child is the Christ child. Then Baboushka goes on her journey, still searching, still knocking, wondering if she will find the Christ child there.

(In one church a woman played her guitar and sang "Baboushka's Carol" as Lenore continued to move down the aisle, ever so slowly, knocking on the pews, searching for the Christ child. Eventually she got to the narthex as the last lines were sung. She turned and knocked loudly on the sanctuary door.)

If you hear someone knocking at your door these days following Christmas and it is Baboushka, how will you respond? Is the Christ child in your heart to abide today and always?

The ideas came from the book Baboushka - A Traditional Russian Folk Tale retold by Arthur Scholey. A Lion Picture Book (text copyright 1982 Arthur Scholey. Lion Publishing Co. 1705 Hubbard Ave. Batavia, Ill 60510). It also has "The Baboushka Carol" that Mr. Scholey wrote.)

Photos used in the book were by author or used by permission of Radovan Grkouski, Jim Moiso, Lisa Burns, Tony Becker, Robert Strong, Richard Litherland and Todd Frimoth.